Become a Successful First-Time CEO

Master the confidence, relationships and strategies you need to succeed

DAVID ROCHE

Re think

First published in Great Britain in 2024
by Rethink Press (www.rethinkpress.com)

© Copyright David Roche

Image credits: Danny Butcher (Chapter 1); WikiImages/
anaterate/garten-gg/David Roche (Chapter 2); VectorMine/
Shutterstock, David Roche 2006 (Chapter 3); David Roche/
Aaron Kennedy 2023 (Chapter 4); ClipArt/David Roche
(Chapter 5); nikitabuida on Freepik (Chapter 6); Wirestock
on Freepik (Chapter 7); David Roche 2023 (Chapter 8); Glen
Ward 2023 (Chapter 9); ClipArt/David Roche (Chapter 10);
Adam Gerrard/The Daily Mirror (Chapter 11); ClipArt/
David Roche (Conclusion)

Cover image © Songquan Deng ǀ Shutterstock

Praise

'I just wish I'd had this as a reference twenty-five years ago.'
— **Glen Ward**, CEO, Syngency

'It's a rarity among business books: incisive, humane and strategic and also a rollicking good read.'
— **Dan Oakey**, Director, Deloitte

'Roche's book reveals that beneath the covers there lurks a sharp and insightful business brain. I learned a lot from working alongside him – and am sure any aspiring leader will too.'
— **David Kohn**, founder and CEO, The Multichannel Expert

'I really enjoyed reading David's book. It's a real source of inspiration and a fountain of advice and knowledge.'
— **Julia Leckey**, founder and former CEO, Honest

'This is not your typical "do this, do that" boring, bullet-pointed business book. David really understands the complexities of becoming an even more successful CEO than you already are. The anecdotes, case studies and wry humour help bring it all alive for me and make it a wonderful and refreshing read. I learned a lot.'
— **Julian Sharples**, CEO, As it is

To Johanna, for both your unwavering support and providing the boot up the backside when required

Contents

PART THREE External Relationships

Foreword

My journey to becoming a CEO started in earnest when I was recruited by and started working with David. We took different paths to the CEO role, but both passionately agree that the support to both attain the role and then succeed within it is really not well defined, nor made widely available. David is ideally placed to fill that void in both this book and through his coaching and mentoring. He engages and writes in a fashion that can resonate with all those that aspire to leading businesses successfully.

I am a chief executive of over twelve years standing with extensive experience within consumer facing digital and physical environments across specialist retail, esports, digital services, gaming events and vast data and insight management within established and startup businesses. I have experience across multiple territories including the US, UK, Ireland, Spain, Scandinavia and Eastern Europe. I built and developed the necessary teams, tech and process infrastructures required for a business to succeed in growth as well as consolidation and restructuring within both public and private environments.

David and I first met when HMV was recruiting for a management role which I had been approached to apply for. Having successfully gained the position, I worked for David as a direct report over three years and we have remained friends since, for over twenty years. Having had a solid start to my career with a top retailer that invested heavily in training and development, I fortunately held several roles that supported building both general management skills and encouraged multi-departmental experience.

David gave me a reality check. He would not have known this at the time, but I realised I had a long way to go if I was to continue to progress. I was initially in awe of his intelligence and the results he drove. It was a completely different environment from the traditional retail I had come from, with a far greater focus on operations and far more political. I witnessed how well David led a highly individual, high-performing team and I know of numerous senior leaders that still rate David highly and enjoyed the times they had working for him. At the same time, David gave me a real confidence and was able to treat individuals very differently to gain the most from their skillset. I realised that if I could make a success of that role with David's support, then I would be well set for further progression.

So, why the book and why David? If you are very focused on your path to becoming a CEO or have just made the leap into your first CEO role, either as part of a plan or somewhat unexpectedly, then David captures many great thoughts, experiences and advice here. David's approach is highly personable – he's the first pick on the team sheet for a night out, with an enviable ability to switch between deep intellectual discussion and side-splitting humour.

David also has a wealth of experience. He has witnessed the great and the awful in leadership and draws on this throughout the book. I was excited that he had put pen to paper to create such a great read and digestible, thought-provoking work for anyone progressing to such a key, but lonely and difficult leadership role.

Martyn Gibbs
Multi-territory retail and gaming services CEO, formerly of Game Digital and Belong Gaming

Introduction

P eople who have reached the top of an organisation are expected to come pre-loaded with all the necessary experience and skills required for the job. New CEOs have typically had a successful career to date and often seem destined for the leading role. In the eyes of others, they may make it look easy and appear to ooze confidence.

But if you are that person, it's likely to feel very different when you turn up at work on day one as a CEO. Over 70% of successful people experience anxiety and impostor syndrome symptoms about their abilities.[1] One day they may be heading a sales and marketing powerhouse department and then the next they are taking on responsibility for the whole company. That means grasping that the post room and reception matter as much as the R&D, HR and legal departments, and that everyone in the company is looking to you for both leadership and their livelihoods. This book is designed to help first-time CEOs entering an existing corporation or organisation. (Startups are slightly different.) It's also full of advice for those aspiring to become first-time CEOs.

Being a CEO is no longer like leading the line and scoring the goals; it's more like wielding the baton as the conductor of an orchestra to bring out the best in each section while ensuring that every contribution is coordinated to deliver the optimum overall outcome.

It's a new skillset and to give yourself the best chance of growing into the role and attaining success you will need encouragement, guidance and nurturing to develop it while on the job. This achievement will confirm you as a good and effective CEO, opening a new level for the rest of your career.

Personally, I consider myself to have been very lucky in my business life. Everyone's definition of 'luck' varies, though. It's clear to me that it is possible to make your own luck. We'll talk more about that in this book as it's a big topic.

I was made a director of a billion-pound turnover company at the age of thirty-three and then CEO of a £220 million entertainment company with 2,000 employees and a million square feet of retail space. A dream job in an industry that I love.

I've been elected president of cross-industry associations, won top awards in the publishing industry and been awarded an honorary fellowship for services to the British book trade. I was also recognised in *The Observer*'s ten most influential individuals in the book industry – one place below a certain JK Rowling!

Currently, I am the chair of two companies as well as providing an exclusive coaching and mentoring service for a few select leaders. Through this service, I have helped bring success to CEOs across a wide range of industries – from academia and publishing to financial services and luxury goods. You may think that your problems are unique but, believe me, the patterns are clear and common across the spectrum.

When promoted to the top job for the first time, it's only natural to have doubts about your ability to succeed in the role.

Specialists feel they lack the general management skills to run a company – many scientific industries have traditionally promoted their most able technicians into senior executive roles without providing the necessary management training.

General managers feel they lack the specialist skills needed in a particular industry – but that's not really a problem. Being a generalist is a specialist skill in itself.

Becoming a CEO for the first time can lead to experiencing stress at an extreme level. Understandable concern that you lack the necessary skills and experience to do the job successfully can morph into a self-fulfilling prophecy and restrict your ability to grow into the role.

What can happen then is:

- You are likely to work twice as hard to overcome the issues, but also procrastinate rather than tackling what you really need to.

- You are often tense about your relationship with your chair, board or investors and are uncertain about how to juggle the focus on improving current performance with developing strategic plans.

- You may worry that your exec team is not completely on board with your appointment and supportive of your direction and priorities for the company.

- All this can be exacerbated by being a new entrant to the sector, little-known by the organisation's clients and partners, and with a minimal reputation within that industry or with the trade media who can amplify your messages and profile.

How can you have the necessary experience to run a company when it's your first time? The word to focus on here is *'necessary'*, so congratulations! You have already ticked this particular box as you have been appointed to the role.

I have worked with many CEOs who look supremely confident to others but are hindered by anxiety. One told me that she was, 'Crippled with fear every working day,' but when, fifteen minutes later, I asked her to tell me about a boss she admired, she said, 'I've never worked for anyone I haven't caught up with and surpassed.' This confidence/crisis combination often compounds the problem. People see an assured façade and assume that you don't need or even want their help.

So, who can you talk to?

That depends on what is going on in your head…

- Your boss gave you the job and wants to know that they made the right decision. You may be worried that asking questions may expose a lack of the required experience that your boss thinks you have – are you a different person to the one they think they hired?

- Some of your direct reports may think they should have got your job. If you were promoted from within, then until your recent appointment, they were your peers and they may not take reporting into you well. If you are external, they may think it should have been an internal appointment.

- You should know all the answers yourself and not need to seek help or advice.

Above all, you feel that you can't show any signs of inexperience or weakness. This can easily develop into a trap: it is comparatively easy to see where others are going wrong and suggest solutions, but it is extremely difficult to self-diagnose these issues and find your own way out.

I have lived through and understand the issues that first-time CEOs face from four sides of the boardroom table: as an executive board member, as a CEO, as a non-exec director (NED) and as the chair. I know that managing and motivating people well is the number one solution that connects all the issues that the novice CEO faces.

Two out of five CEOs fail in their first eighteen months according to the *Harvard Business Review*,[2] and it's not their expertise or experience to blame; it's their people skills, political nous and inability to build the necessary relationships with the key points of contact in the company.

Through my company, Grey Area Coaching Ltd, I have devised the CEO Winner's Circle. This is an eight-step process that concentrates on *You* throughout. It shows you how to not just manage, but also to take the lead with the key relationships you need to master:

- Your relationship with yourself:
  - How you think about and deal with yourself
- Internal relationships:
  - Upwards, with your chair, board and investors
  - With your direct reports
  - Across the overall organisation that you now run
- External relationships:
  - With clients and suppliers
  - With partners
  - Across the wider industry
  - With the media

These steps will give you the tools to improve each of these relationships and get everyone pulling in the same direction. Their success leads to the company's success – which leads to your success. You can never get rid of office politics completely, but you can make relationships work for you and for the good of the organisation. The resulting reduction in stress and angst will help you to enjoy your job and also have a dramatic and beneficial effect on your home life.

When your problems seem insurmountable, the solution can appear miraculous. I have seen it work for me and for the CEOs that I work with. The first CEO client that I helped with this approach wrote a testimonial declaring, 'David's coaching sessions have had a profound impact on my life.'

This book is designed for first-time CEOs, or those aspiring to become one, who know that they don't have all the answers, but are unsure where to find the much-needed support that they need. Perhaps someone like you. It has case studies on how people like you have learned to succeed and has anecdotes that may trigger ideas in your own mind that answer your immediate needs. In my coaching and mentoring sessions with first-time CEOs, it is remarkable how discussing a real example from my own past can unlock a parallel problem my current client is wrestling with – not with exactly the same answer, but often with a lightbulb moment that helps them see their own issue differently.

This is not a 'be like me' book from a once-in-a-generation, superstar business guru whose advice may be admirable, but difficult (if not impossible) for the rest of us to pull off. It's also not for narcissists who are happy to bulldoze their way to the top without worrying about the damage caused to others or the organisation along the way. It's for every first-time and aspiring CEO who wants to increase their chances of doing well in their job and bringing success to their company and its people.

I believe passionately that professional, independent coaching and mentoring should become compulsory for all first-time CEOs. It's a relatively minor investment, with a major long-term payback, both commercially and personally. The world is in need of great leaders. This is my contribution towards shaping the next generation of outstanding, empathetic leaders with both the vision and high emotional intelligence to achieve amazing things.

PART ONE
YOU

ONE
It's All About You

*Overcoming hesitation and embracing
your inner captain*

> 'To be yourself in a world that is constantly
> trying to make you something else is the
> greatest accomplishment.'
>   — Ralph Waldo Emerson

On 8 May 2006, Guy Goma visited BBC Television Centre in West London to attend an interview for a junior position in the BBC's IT department. He was sitting in reception when one of the BBC News 24 producers came along and asked if his name was Guy. When he said yes, he was taken to the studio, made up, mic'd up and then seated in front of the cameras. He simply assumed that this was how the BBC conducted its job interviews.

Karen Bowerman, the news interviewer, then introduced him on air as Guy Kewney, editor of the technology website, Newswireless. Guy Goma's face revealed all: he was live on TV and he was supposed to be an expert on the topic he was being asked about. In the best traditions of Chauncey Gardner in the Peter Sellers film *Being There*,[3] when Guy expressed his surprise, it was taken out of context and presumed to be an authoritative opinion on the 'Apple Corps v Apple Computer' High Court ruling that day. Growing in confidence, Guy then predicted that the ease of downloading would likely see it dominating the future; he was thanked for his input and the live broadcast interview ended.[4]

Sadly, his subsequent interview for the data position that he had come for lasted not much longer and he didn't get the job. He did, however, become an overnight sensation and was invited onto many shows and interviews. He returned to the news in August 2023, threatening to sue the BBC for lack of royalties for a clip that has been watched over five million times.[5]

Guy Goma's TV appearance was a perfect example of what you might call reverse impostor syndrome – being thought qualified to talk about something when you are not. Once he realised his predicament was the result of mistaken identity, he probably experienced FOBFO (Fear of Being Found Out) and must have thought, 'There's no way I can pull this off!', but he rose to the challenge and, amazingly, it worked. His journey during those one-and-a-bit minutes in the spotlight can take others decades to navigate over their careers.

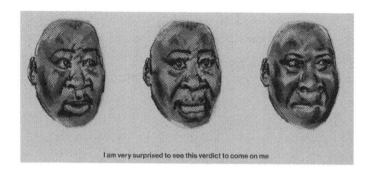

I am very surprised to see this verdict to come on me

The surprised faces of Guy Goma as captured
by illustrator Danny Butcher

Unsurprisingly, in our own heads, everything revolves around ourselves. It's all about 'me'. Others who exhibit a certain level of competence and confidence that is at odds with how we believe we can contribute may come into our orbit and interact with us, but we are the one constant and see everything from our own point of view.

How to be ready to take on more responsibility

When a professional rugby player is whacked on the head, they are given an HIA (Head Injury Assessment) with various protocols to assess whether the player is concussed, or worse. One such protocol involves being asked (hopefully) obvious questions. When these 'Maddocks Questions'[6] were originally devised, they were along the lines of, 'Who is the Prime Minister?' (Admittedly, this was before the Johnson/

Truss/Sunak carousel.) The goal of the questions is to check that our points of reference are in place and our memory and logic are unimpaired. In short, that we are fit and able to give of our best and perform well.

A first-time CEO experiences the reverse of this. They are taken out of their comfort – and sometimes competence – zone and put into an unfamiliar position of overall responsibility that they have not experienced before to this degree. This is most often performed without providing the support and coaching that are designed to ensure that they will execute to the best of their ability. In fact, the likelihood is that there will be a lack of confidence or some doubt that will hold the new CEO back and may impair their functioning.

Why wouldn't everyone be doing their utmost to ensure that the person filling the most important position in the company is given the optimum support to succeed in the role?

It may be easy to see this as an observer, but it doesn't look that way for most people who take up the company reins for the first time. What tends to be going through their head is:

- I'm supposed to be good enough or I wouldn't have been given the job.

- I'm supposed to have all the answers as I'm the person running the company.

- Everyone is expecting me to know what to do, to give my opinion and to make the right decisions.

This is pressure, and for most, it is at a level that they've never experienced before. Everyone in the company depends on you. And their families and dependants do too. Their livelihood depends on the success of the company, and, therefore, on you.

I remember this feeling well when I started my first-time CEO role. My previous job had been as a functional head – a board director with big responsibilities that contributed directly to the commercial success of the company. I worked for the major high street retailer HMV and ran the product (or buying) department that decided what ranges we carried in our hundreds of stores, negotiated how much we paid our suppliers and determined the price and campaigns we used to entice our customers. I had over sixty staff in my department and naively believed that I was the most important contributor among my fellow board directors (and, on several occasions, more so than the MD). I'm sure many of my colleagues on the board felt the same about their own positions. I was confident in both my contribution and my ability to deliver successfully in the role. I then moved to Waterstones (spelled Waterstone's when I joined the company) and performed the same role for three years. Both companies were prosperous and number one in the industry. My working life was good, but I wanted more.

My first-time CEO role was in a (still) large and respected rival in the same industry. Borders was a popular US brand that had successfully infiltrated the UK market by acquiring the predominantly London-based chain BOOKS etc, and was expanding quickly. Suddenly, every member of its staff would be looking to me for their inspiration and livelihood. The people on reception and in the post room were as important as the CFO and head of marketing and I was as responsible for one as to the other.

I was based in London and my bosses were in Michigan in the US, on Eastern time, five hours behind. I had been approached by them while I was officially on gardening leave following my resignation from my previous role. This had been a complicated and slightly messy exit (more of which later) and I was delighted not only to be contacted by this organisation, but also to have the time to do some real research on them and put in the best possible application for the CEO role. This resulted in many site visits and calculated (and what turned out to be correct) assumptions that resulted from an identification and examination of every major business area – viewed from the outside. On the basis of what I saw, I produced a comprehensive report that listed what I believed to be the issues and weaknesses that the company displayed in its offer, the likely causes in processes and systems, and an action plan to address each of them and secure the company's success in the future. I also proposed ten quick wins that could be implemented in the first 100 days.

I sent this report to the US prior to getting on the plane for my second series of interviews. I arrived in a snow storm and suffering from a streaming cold and the drive across Michigan from Detroit to Ann Arbor in the hire car in a blizzard left me pretty whacked. The next day I had five one-hour interviews with the company president, my boss-to-be and various main board members. There was no break between each, and I conducted these with a runny nose, a box of tissues on the table and a bin between my knees. However, I could tell early on that despite this, it was going well and was likely to lead to me being offered the new role of UK & Ireland CEO. As it turned out, the report I had prepared in advance was exceptionally well received and had convinced them that I knew what I was doing before many of them had even met me.

On starting the CEO role a couple of months later, I had a big advantage that a lot of first-time CEOs don't have: a plan of action which I understood and backed, and that already had the approval of my US bosses. I now had to get to know the business and its people to ensure that my plan would work in reality – and not just on paper.

One would think that this advantage would instil a sense of confidence in the position that I now found myself in and in my ability to perform well. To a certain extent it did, but it was still an uneasy ride at the beginning. My bosses were overseas and wanted not just a 'hockey stick' three-year plan, but for that year's budget to immediately deliver a profit from a business that had been in investment and expansion mode and delivering losses. Having demanding bosses who ask for probably unrealistic turnarounds in too short timeframes is the way of the world, but that doesn't make it any easier when the person responsible for delivering it all is you.

What can happen then is that you enter a procrastination loop. You are trying to meet as many people as possible in your organisation. You are also meeting with your clients and partners to establish where you sit with them. You may undertake some research with your consumers as to how you and your products or services are perceived. And you may be being pursued by the trade media to find out a bit more about you and what your plan is for the business. Or you may just be trying to confirm whether it's better to spell 'impostor' with an 'o' or an 'e' at the end...

In my case I already had my list of things to do from the already approved 100-day-plan, and the verification I conducted of the proposals it contained happened relatively quickly. Throughout my career, and particularly when I have been doing consulting, I have been able to put my finger quickly on where the problem is and what needs addressing. Creating and implementing the plan to address this takes a little longer and requires buy-in from those who are delegated the responsibility to deliver it.

At this point, it can be easy to fall into the trap of seeking further verification beyond the point where it is necessary. When interviewing staff members, it doesn't take long to establish a pattern and hear a consistent story of what the problem is. You might talk to more than one hundred people, but you probably have a relatively clear picture after speaking to the first ten. As a consultant paid by the hour, talking to one hundred people and then writing up your report and recommendations may be the sensible, if self-interested, way of going about this. As the CEO, it's far better to start addressing the situation as early as possible. Roger Mavity, ex-CEO of Granada's Leisure and Technology Divisions and the Conran Group, and author of *The Rule Breaker's Book of Business: Win at work by doing things differently* (which I agented), likes to say, 'A bad decision on Monday makes more money than a good decision on Friday.'[7] As the leader of the company, people will expect you to lead and that means making decisions rather than dithering. Listen to your inner captain who has assessed the information and position and knows the best course of action; demonstrate your able captaincy.

Seeing the wood among the trees

If you were to see a colleague or friend in a similar position, the chances are that you would be able to give them good advice as to what their best course of action should be, but when it's about you and your situation, people can find it incredibly difficult to see what the best route is. You can't see the wood for the trees.

This is where a professional, independent coach/ mentor comes in. A coach will ask you the right questions to allow you to unlock yourself from the situation that is binding you and impairing your decision-making. A mentor may help you with advice from their greater experience as to what is likely to work best under the circumstances – but they may be wrong. Coaches may frown on the deviation from the 'questions only' approach, but they may lack the relevant experience to adopt mentoring. Even if you have the experience, getting this balance right is a complex skill, but invaluable when done well. A talented and experienced coach/mentor not only helps the individual they are supporting to find their own best route, but can provide practical advice at the same time.

Independence is critical, especially when the problem at this point for the new CEO boils down to this: *It is all about me!*

The fact that the CEO is thinking, 'I am the problem,' means that they can't share any of this with anyone else at work. They are in the FOBFO stage. Daunted by the 'Fear Of Being Found Out', their doubts say, 'I'm not sure that I'm good enough to do this job and it's only a matter of time before everyone else finds out.'

When you are seemingly on your own, in the middle of the stress, pressure and loneliness that being at the top can bring, it is nigh on impossible to see a way to leap into a world of excellent relationships and high performance.

Nobody tells you what being a CEO really entails: the fact it will take over and dominate your life morning, noon and night; that your family may have to take a bit of a back seat as it consumes your waking hours, and that this requires an understanding and agreement with those outside of work in order to keep your home life intact and free you to concentrate on work. You may lose control over areas of expertise that you used to run, only to take on additional areas with which you are unfamiliar. You are only human. The demands on your time are remorseless and come from both inside and outside the company. Nobody, not even you, can perform brilliantly, or even well, at everything.

The pressure on CEOs to produce the desired results, and quickly, is also consistent. There are plenty of books, blogs and podcasts that throw out top tips, for example:

- Listen twice as much as you speak (two ears, one mouth...).

- Be approachable.

- Build a culture of risk-taking without blame.

- Understand that you don't have the answers to everything yourself.

- Adopt a consistent leadership model.

- Embrace change and adaptability.

- Focus on the long haul.

- Have an honest, two-way relationship with your boss.

For some of these, the ball is in your court, but what if your boss does not encourage the sort of relationship that some of these suggest and demands instant results instead?

It is the ability to get the best out of each and every one of your relationships, both inside and outside the company, that will provide the launchpad for success. This is what we will be examining from every angle to provide support in making this happen. CEOs are human, after all, despite everyone looking to them for the vision and solutions, and they will make mistakes despite the perception (their own) that this is unacceptable.

I have talked to and interviewed many, many CEOs during the course of my work. The surprise is how many of them experienced the exact same doubts and concerns at the beginning of their career. You've got the job, you're more than capable of doing it well and there's a mountain of evidence that you are good enough at what you have done. You just need to do what you can to ensure the transition is a success.

It is also worth giving thought to your personal leadership rules. Do you want to be the same type of person as a CEO as you are in the rest of your life, as opposed to the way you think a CEO is supposed to be? Anyone who has watched the TV series *Succession* will have recoiled from the leadership examples portrayed by the Roy family.[8] Eugene Buckley, the co-founder of Calculum Inc, said this to me about the CEO position itself: 'It tends to attract the "Super Alpha" types, which all too often turn into sociopath "All hail, Caesar" personalities, or creates a culture of sycophancy.' Most of us will have worked at some point in time for a boss who wasn't great, and some of those will have been towards the caricature end of the scale.

It just doesn't have to be that way for you when you are a CEO. If you are yourself, then you will come across as genuine and remove the pressure of constantly trying to put on an act.

Keynote takeaway

If it is all about just you, then find another pair of eyes to help you with perspective and to provide support. Bear in mind that your relationship with others is just a variable and a reaction to your own outlook. As the next chapter will show, luckily, it really isn't all about just you.

TWO

It's All About Everyone Else Too

Most CEOs have a similar journey to find success and sanity

'If a man will begin with certainties, he shall end in doubts, but if he will be content to begin with doubts, he shall end in certainties.'
— Francis Bacon

The talented writer Neil Gaiman tells a wonderful story about being invited to attend a convention along with other creators, inventors, scientists and celebrities. When he was there, he was hit hard with concerns that he wasn't deserving of being included in such a commendable circle of attendees and that he would be found out as unworthy. At an evening event, he found himself talking to a much older gentleman who shared both the same first name and the concerns about being worthy to attend the convention.

The old boy said: 'I just look at all these people, and I think, what the heck am I doing here? They've made amazing things. I just went where I was sent.' Neil Gaiman responded: 'Yes. But you were the first man on the moon. I think that counts for something.'[9] If Neil Armstrong could suffer from impostor syndrome, then we all can.

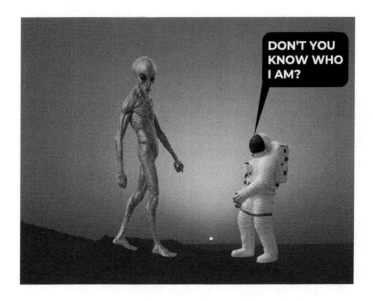

Impostor syndrome is reassuringly common

Michelle Obama is quoted as saying she still feels 'imposter syndrome – it never goes away.'[10] Howard Schultz, the former chairman and CEO of Starbucks, said, 'Very few people, whether you've been in that job before or not, get into the seat and believe today that they are now qualified to be the CEO. They're not going to tell you that, but it's true.'[11]

This chapter explores how widespread the problem that you may be experiencing with personal stress actually is.

Everyone is winging it to a greater or lesser extent

Most of us have doubts about our experience and ability and do our utmost to disguise this. That makes it difficult for others to see the need to provide support. The reverse of the 'can't see the wood for the trees' issue also applies here: the majority of people have anxiety about their own position but can't easily spot this as common among others. Research for NerdWallet in 2022 showed that 78% of business leaders experience workplace impostor syndrome, causing 59% to consider leaving their role.[12]

The interesting question to ask is what about those rare individuals that do not suffer from any doubts or lack of confidence – the ones who think they are always right and don't require any consultation or feedback before acting?

On the day that Liz Truss became Prime Minister in September 2022, she and her Chancellor Kwasi Kwarteng sacked Sir Tom Scholar, the experienced and respected permanent secretary at the Treasury. She had a blueprint for growth to mollify the far-right wing of the Conservative Party who had been responsible for her elevation to the role. What she did not want was negative feedback about her strategy or an assessment or independent advice on the potential damage it may cause to the economy. The resulting plan was called a 'mini-budget' in order to avoid the Office for Budget Responsibility's independent forecasts and formal scrutiny that accompany a 'budget'. As it turned out, Truss' plan was a disaster, and billions were wiped off the economy as a result. Supreme confidence can deliver spectacular results in either direction.[13]

What this behaviour can also discourage is the willingness of those around such a confident leader to speak truth to power, as such advice is not received well. Any alteration to the scheme is viewed as implied criticism and unwelcome. We all tend to gravitate towards echo chambers and our world is increasingly binary. The encouragement of debate, acceptance of differing viewpoints and the ability to step into others' shoes and empathise is increasingly rare, but these are part of the armoury of the highly skilled leader – in business, as well as politics

The Dunning-Kruger Effect[14] reflects the relationship between confidence and experience. As we've seen in the example above, a lack of knowledge and skills can lead to an overestimation of one's own competence – one's ability to do a job. There is also a byproduct to this whereby those who do excel in an area assume that it is also simple for everyone else and fail to recognise their own skill and experience.

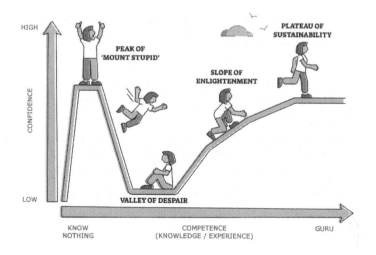

The bliss of ignorance – the Dunning-Kruger Effect

Help works best when those who need it, welcome it. Given the option of supreme confidence versus impostor syndrome-driven caution, there is at least the opportunity to change and develop if you suffer from the latter.

One of the common but incorrect assumptions of impostor syndrome is that it is a female-only characteristic, partly developed as a result of glass ceilings and mansplaining in the male-dominated higher echelons of business. In their book *The Confidence Code: The science and art of self-assurance – what women should know*,[15] authors and TV broadcasters Katty Kay and Claire Shipman put this down to women's relatively lower confidence and the connected impairment in their promotion and recruitment prospects as a result of a lack of blowing their own trumpets. Another view is that women are penalised for acting in the same self-promoting way that self-confident males do to get ahead. I was told by Tuula Ingman, a highly regarded specialist orthodontist and CEO of Ingman-Med, that in Finland they have a great word: *turvallisuuden-hakuinen*. My understanding is that this means, at one level, security-oriented – but not so much in a risk-averse way; it also incorporates a tendency to stand back from the limelight – to not push oneself forwards to take the credit. Again, this perhaps applies more to women than to men, and affects the numbers who put themselves forward in either applications or in meta-phorically putting their hands up all the time.

These reasons are all valid and the perceived causes need to be eradicated, but this does not mean that men do not suffer from impostor syndrome – and they certainly suffer from the associated stress when put under pressure. I am not advocating greater sym-pathy for men as a result – far from it. I have seen unfair and downright awful treatment of women at work over the years and, without a doubt, the best bosses I have had have been women.

Specialists specialise

In the journey to the top of organisations, it has often been the case in the past that the most competent person in their specialist role gets promoted to a higher job, quite possibly involving more management responsibility.

The most talented chemists, the most successful engineers, the best teachers – they're elevated from their peers and, generally along their upward journey, moved further from the roles where they demonstrated the most skill. Do their specialist skills translate automatically into management and executive competence? No. Will they enjoy their new roles in the same way that they did when mastering their work? Not necessarily. Should pay rates for particular expertise enable those experts to stay in their roles if they choose to and become world class at what they do? Probably.

In the late seventeenth and early eighteenth century, Stradivari created incredible string instruments – mainly violins – and he is renowned as the best ever at doing what he did. He had a shop in Cremona, Italy, but I suspect he didn't feel the need to open Stradivarius Superstores all over the world or diversify into woodwind or brass instruments. He just produced the best product he could and kept refining the design and process to try and make them even better.

Can specialists be trained and developed to become great general managers and CEOs? Yes, of course.

General management is a specialist skill

General management is a specialist skill in its own right and should be recognised as such. Of course, those general managers who have not come up through the specialist route may suffer doubts about lacking the specialist expertise and experience to excel in their jobs. However, they do have the knowledge that they need diversified teams with specialist skills to achieve success.

Later in one's career, generalisation may be recognised more openly as a valued skill. As chair of London Book Fair, I bring many years of running bookstore chains, working at the top of multinational publishing, contributing as a NED and trustee in the book world, having acted as the literary agent for a number of successful authors, and being a published writer myself. This is not seen as an unfocused career path but rather an all-round set of experiences that make me suitable for the role.

Had I chosen to remain as a retail CEO, in order to progress I would probably have had to change industries to another that the retailer operated in. To have taken on the running of a supermarket chain or a shoe-shop empire may have been seen by some as progression, but it was not something that I wished to do. In my case, the world of publishing was a wonderful discovery and followed on naturally from the world of music, films and games where I cut my teeth. It is seductive and kept me in its orbit, as it does to many who work in it and attest the same. But at the beginning, it's a learning curve that comes with the same doubts and insecurities as any other industry.

Recognising impostor syndrome

There are many taxonomies of impostor syndrome that sort people into boxes. The acknowledged authority on the subject is Dr Valerie Young and it's likely that she originated the different types. I highly advise reading her excellent book, *The Secret Thoughts of Successful Women: Why capable people suffer from the impostor syndrome and how to thrive in spite of it* – for men as well as women.[16] These categories have their uses, but I find that people may belong in more than one category. Here are the typically identified types and some thoughts to accompany them:

The Natural Genius

We all know the type – a natural at everything they attempt to do and one who succeeds from the off without the practice and effort that the rest of us need to put in to be half as good. As a result, they believe they should get things right first time, whether that is completing tasks or picking up new skills. When this doesn't happen, this leads to confusion and questioning whether they are as good as they thought, or quite possibly, as others thought. If at first, they don't succeed, then WTF?

Anyone who plays golf will know someone who effortlessly plays to a very low handicap even though they don't get out on the course (or the range) very often. It's really irritating for those of us who put the hours in, master the game on the range ironing out all those kinks in our swing, only to be unable to replicate it on the course when it matters – in some cases, letting a minor setback dominate our thinking and leading to a mental collapse and disintegration of the game.

When you are not a natural genius yourself, it's difficult to observe any weakness and doubt in those that are. Natural geniuses are people others wish they were or whose skills are desirable, so how could they possibly have doubts or need help themselves?

People suffering from the natural genius impostor syndrome mindset may also be perpetually disappointed by the people they work with and report to – which isn't exactly the bedrock of a successful relationship with them. They would benefit from understanding that training, learning and practising lead to growth and improvement. Everyone benefits from this and they will profit from working with a coach/mentor despite a natural inclination to recoil from such a suggestion.

The Perfectionist

This group have no time for second best or good enough. It has to be perfect every time. That is just not going to happen, so they are setting themselves up for a fall. When they do well, they focus on the small mistakes that detracted from the perfect rather than the vast majority that went well.

They may deliver a great speech that carries the room, but they know they stumbled at the beginning of one line and left out what they believed to be a key point in the middle. No one else noticed and their oratory skills and arguments achieved the aim, but it in their own mind it could have been better.

The Perfectionist may struggle to delegate to others as they believe they will do it better themselves. However, they may not attempt something new if they feel they won't get it perfectly right off the bat. They may also delay action, such as making a decision, pushing the button on an activity, or releasing a product as it's not perfect, so not ready. This is a mistake, as we know that testing in the market is the best way to improve and secure long-term success.

The Perfectionist would benefit from understanding that a minimum viable product – 'good enough quality', if you like – is quicker, cheaper and better than perfect. Again, it's not easy to see them as lacking confidence and, therefore, requiring help, but it will benefit them.

Many of us will attest to the fact that we learn most from both our and others' mistakes, so making them is a crucial part of the development process.

The Superhero

These individuals do not just succeed at work, but across all their roles in life and with all they encounter, be that work, family, friends or acquaintances. Unlike the natural genius, they believe this is all as a result of the effort that they put in. They have to work harder in order to overcome their lack of innate ability. Any failure means that they didn't try hard enough and raises their concern that it should be easier if they really were good enough. They may have qualifications coming out of their ears but Masters degrees, Doctorates, MBAs and industry accolades still don't mean they know enough.

This person works hard in order not to let the team down and to progress on behalf of themselves and their family. They may also volunteer for the neighbourhood support groups and a local charity helping the community. One of their kids may play for the local football team and so they are taking coaching lessons to help the team; the other kid is a competitive swimmer who needs a lift to the pool at the crack of dawn for their practice. They also drive to see their elderly parents every weekend and help them with their shopping.

Superheroes believe they have to work far harder than everyone else in order to succeed. They also may be loading the system in an unsustainable way.

They need to understand that there is a level beyond which any more effort or hours will make little or no difference. Also, that others' comments can be constructive and not critical, implied or otherwise. And they need to learn to say no – a crucial skill for anyone; ask those who have left corporate work and set up their own business as a freelancer or consultant.

The Soloist

The Soloist is not a team player and has a preference for working on their own. This also plays heavily with first-time CEOs who believe that as the new top dog, they should have the ability to answer all the questions and solve all the problems. They are worried that seeking help and advice from others can be perceived as a weakness and may compensate by putting in even more hours and effort in an attempt to overcome their limitations.

The vibe that you work best alone rubs off on others and this rejection of offers of help means others leave you to it.

It's a circular process that will lead to even greater isolation. The problem is also two-way in that you feel you can't go to others for help, and they back off from giving support that you so badly need. This is a classic example of where an independent coach/mentor can really make a dramatic difference. You need to locate and identify the right people to ask for help and work with.

The Expert

The Expert is really into the detail and needs to know all there is to know about something to succeed at it. This can lead to procrastination as there is always more to learn. Even though they may be considered an expert already, this is not enough for them. They may also not apply for new positions or jobs as they don't tick every single box for skills and experience needed when such a candidate just doesn't exist.

These Experts would benefit from getting into the habit of focused, just-in-time learning only applied when needed; only deep-diving as and when it is strictly necessary. Experts benefit from the realisation of just how much they do know. Mentoring more junior colleagues, lecturing at vocational courses and becoming a NED or trustee can all be areas which both help others and boost their own confidence.

What this teaches us

Rather than pigeonholing everyone with impostor syndrome labels, I believe that people can move between, or overlap across, the groups depending on the topic, their circumstances and the group of people around them. A CEO may be an excellent public speaker and communicator, but as a Perfectionist they may tinker with the text as it's never perfect. It's possible that they do this at the expense of rehearsing it properly, which means both structurally with an eye on content and in a performance sense so that the emphasis and timing are as they need to be. This may lead to a couple of hiccoughs on the day that the Perfectionist will absolutely hate but which the audience may not even notice.

The common factor across all the impostor syndrome types is that others may not notice that you are anything other than confident and be totally unaware that you require help. Impostor syndrome is a very personal thing. Even if most of us suffer from it to some degree, we don't recognise that the majority of others do too. We should, therefore, look out for it when people are promoted or take up senior positions for the first time.

Self-policing and self-help work too. Eric Partaker is a well-regarded CEO coach and his advice about impostor syndrome is to consider, 'Would it hold up in court?'[17] And if not, to build a case file of evidence and repeat it as a mantra daily to remind yourself of your value. I understand that some people can be a bit 'meh' about having confirmation statements pinned up at work and think of it all as a bit Steve Coogan's Gareth Cheeseman character growling, 'I'm a Tiger!' into a mirror before his sales pitch.[18] The important thing is to recognise your worth, your experience and your skills and that these contribute to attaining the best results. It's not down to luck, and it's not down solely to others – managing a team, recognising others' strengths and playing to them are highly valuable skills in themselves.

Keynote takeaway

It's clear that the majority of first-time CEOs suffer from some degree of impostor syndrome, but not all of them are as effective as they could be at managing and overcoming it. Help is at hand with a professional, independent coach/mentor. First-time CEOs need to recognise their doubts as commonplace, build their confidence and act on the transition areas that they can control themselves.

THREE

CEO Swagger

Cultivating unshakeable confidence at the helm

'One secret of success in life is for a man to be
ready for his opportunity when it comes.'
— Benjamin Disraeli

Twenty-five years or so ago, when I was younger
and possibly more foolish, my wife and I were
taking a morning flight from Delhi to Beijing on
Ethiopian Airways. As we boarded the plane, we
were faced with gaffer tape across the facing door and
handwritten signs that read: 'Please Don't Operate
This Door' and 'Do Not Open'. We were also met by a
large group of very unhappy Chinese fellow passengers who were milling around in the aisle, pointing at
the door and refusing to sit down.

My pre-smartphone snap of the dodgy sign
on a flight back in 2006

I asked one of the attendants what was going on and they explained that the emergency chute would not work on that door should we be forced to crash land, but the plane had flown in from Addis Ababa and they were happy it was safe to fly to Beijing. That was the plan, but the Chinese contingent weren't having any of it.

After about fifteen minutes more of this I said to my wife, 'This plane is going nowhere. I'm going to do something.' I approached the lead flight attendant and the self-declared spokesperson and translator for the Chinese passengers. In my best, reassuring pilot's voice I said, 'Hello, my name is David Roche, and I'm an aircraft designer working for Boeing in London. What you need to know is that the cabin pressure at altitude will press the door against the fuselage, making a catastrophic door failure impossible.' The Chinese lady nodded and translated for her fellow passengers. They all nodded and took their seats, and then we were off.

'God,' my wife said, 'if we do go down, I hope we don't survive to be sued...' An hour or more later, the captain came back to talk to us. 'Lucky, we had an aircraft designer on board!' he smiled. I responded, 'I don't know the first thing about aircraft, but if you can keep a secret and some free drinks coming, no one else need know.'

This example is purely to illustrate that you don't need to know a lot about something to kid others that you do. Outright lying is not a great idea in any circumstances. The point is, it's amazing what confidence and a bit of resulting swagger can do. If you act the part, you're more likely to be accepted as someone worthy of the role.

Making your own luck

In business, particularly around promotions and appointments, there's a lot of talk about luck – generally from the people who were passed over for the role. The successful candidate may well be putting it down to luck too, but they are less likely to be saying so, or even giving off that vibe. And it generally isn't luck, either. Even if you happen to be in the right place at the right time, you still need to have done the groundwork and preparation to anticipate where the right place might be and when the right time is.

In the past, CEOs were more likely than now to be appointed after a tap on the shoulder or given opportunities not shared with the wider company. It was maybe even potentially a done deal, with possibly a rubber stamp interview. There was likely to have been self-justification as to why the 'lucky' individual had been selected – it's never declared as nepotism. Rather than favouritism, it is considered to be earned on the basis of the work done before, good results and the ensuing trust that this instilled in the future boss that this was someone who was smart and could learn, could be relied on and would be a good fit for the role and in the team.

The person with ambition should demonstrate curiosity about the entire business rather than just their own field of expertise. Understanding all key areas, such as IT, rights, property, how the CFO assesses risk and success, etc. This will develop a real knowledge of how departments, teams and individuals operate cohesively. The more evidence of these traits you can provide, the 'luckier' you can become.

The best candidates are ready for the right role to come along, even if they don't know it is coming.

A focus on luck also obscures the need to develop your own team and a choice of capable successors. Rather than worrying about creating a rival who may want and eventually take your job, the right approach is to nurture your replacement so that your own promotion will be easy and risk-free. How many times have you seen someone stuck in the job because they were 'irreplaceable'? It's not necessarily fair, but in a close call between them and someone else, it can become a factor. As CEO, when you believe it's time to move on to another company, the lack of a successor can act as a handbrake if you believe you owe a debt to the company and stakeholders. As with many big decisions in life, there is never the perfect time to push the button.

This preparedness is critical, no matter where you are on the corporate ladder. In the early days, it may be as a result of being able to move location as necessary or take advantage of a new technical development or way of working. The early social media marketers were a great example of this, and these roles provided a big opportunity for new entrants to previously difficult-to-enter industries. Right at the beginning of my career, I worked for an American textile producer in their production planning department. There was a clear hierarchy that had been established, and it was based on length of service. Then it was announced that the whole production and sales forecasting practices and processes were to be computerised and the ledgers and antiquated, slightly intuitive, processes were to be binned. This provided a wonderful opportunity for me to leapfrog many of the longer serving team in the space of a few weeks. I was not stuck in the same tramlines as those who had performed the same functions for, in some cases, more than a decade and who dreaded the change.

The willingness to embrace change and jump in the deep end with little direct experience is essential if you want to progress. Opportunities may not be linear and may be lateral. After being hired by HMV in 1989 as operations manager until being recruited as chief executive at Borders in 2006, I had several jobs and was invited to take them on without the job being advertised. This was partly as the roles had not been fully specified at the time but were developmental; including both the roles mentioned here, every job I had between 1986 and 2008 was a brand-new position that didn't exist before I took on the role.

At the time there certainly seemed to me to be plenty of upsides to this. On the impostor side, there was no proven expectation as to what the role could achieve and there was no track record from a previous incumbent that one had to match. On the more creative side, one could make the job into what you wanted.

Yes, there were outcomes that you needed to deliver, but the exact detail of *how* was generally left to you – the Harry Enfield character whose catchphrase is, 'You don't wanna do it like that...' was nowhere to be seen.[19]

You need to be ready. There will always be the question of who has the right experience for the role, who has the best aptitude, who has the right character and who is the best fit. There's bound to be a bit of give and take on these, as it's unlikely one person is at the top of all these ladders. If we assume that all the candidates' experience is sufficient, the most important factor is then likely to be attitude.

It's not so much, 'Can they do it?' It's more, 'Can they be trusted to do it?'

If an individual's attitude is right, you know they will do everything that they can to achieve success on behalf of the company, will liaise with colleagues as necessary to secure engagement and make the right calls, will keep their boss appraised of progress (thus eliminating any surprises where possible) and present potential solutions and reasons when obstacles are encountered. Delivering any strategy involves change, and these elements are vital in securing a good outcome and provide a base for the best communication to flow from. Be that person.

Learning from experience

There are two other things to bear in mind as your career progresses and opportunities present themselves. They are connected with how you react to opportunities as they arise, and how you handle your situation if they don't go your way. I certainly have felt the disappointment more than once of not getting a particular promotion that I thought at the time would be massively beneficial to my career. These are entirely attitudinal.

The first is that everything happens for a reason. You should learn from disappointments so that when the next opportunity comes along, you are better positioned to take advantage of it. If you are an optimist with a positive attitude, you may also believe that a particular thing didn't happen because something even better is round the corner. When I was in a middle management position at HMV, there was a job going as the business development manager at the parent company, HMV Group. This was the small management team that developed the strategy for international expansion and managed the collective accounts and financing for the Group. Despite it being a similar level, I believed that this role devising strategy and assessing new markets would be a move in the right direction and I was very disappointed to just miss out on the job. However, being in an operating company at the sharp end turned out to be a much better route to the top. Within a year, I had managed to get a directorship on the UK board, the biggest operating company the Group had.

They key to getting that position was demonstrating both competence and confidence in equal measure which inspired enough trust to take the risk of giving me the responsibility for a newly created role. Once again, there was a major project undertaken and the entire company's systems were being updated. These included the finance systems, tills and cash systems in all the stores, the stock control across the millions of individual lines the company stocked and sold, as well as the pipes that would link all these together and the training to utilise it all. I was put in charge of this massive project which, if successful, would enable HMV to expand at a rate that would see us become the market leader by some distance. It was seen by some as a bit of a hospital pass; the IT director was handing the project over to operations for the implementation phase, and the ops director was shovelling it on to me to deliver. A great opportunity, still.

It was critical, but it was also very detailed and not the most interesting at that level for many of those at the top of the company. I learned early on that printing out dozens of pages of the massive and complex PERT chart (Program Evaluation and Review Technique) and stitching them together across a large wall in the project office was invaluable. If the Group chairman or MD of the company came to check how everything was going, I would immediately jump up and offer to explain where we were on our journey, how we had got there and where we were going next. This was always met with a, 'Jolly good, er, carry on...' response. I learned the hard and valuable skills of project management, but I also learned a lot about managing upwards during this assignment.

The second lesson was also a hard one to learn. When I was Product Director at Waterstones, I had helped rebuild our relationship with the publishers and agents and we won the Bookselling Chain of the Year at the British Book Awards for the first time in a while. I had also just been appointed as president of the key industry body, The Booksellers Association. Waterstones had experienced a rotating door for their MDs, with the HMV Group COO and former HMV MD stepping in as interim MD for the third time as he tried, once again, to find the right MD to take the UK's largest book chain forward. There had been mixed success for those who had moved from HMV into their now sister company, Waterstones. The bookshop chain's stores were very different in their operational capability, urgency, culture and basic academic curiosity. They required a different sort of hand on the tiller. At this point I felt I had proved myself and was ready. I was invited to a dinner in Barnes in south west London that I will never forget. I was told that it had been decided that I would be given the Waterstones' MD job, and it would be announced in a couple of months' time in the new year.

Naturally, I was delighted, determined to work my socks off to make the company perform well and just a little daunted. When I discussed this confidentially with a former boss and previous MD who had moved back to HMV, I was advised to keep on track as I had been doing, be patient and wait for the appointment to be announced. On Christmas Eve, I was assured by him that all was still good. In the new year, I was called to a meeting at HMV Group which I assumed was the confirmation meeting and was told that there had been a change of mind and the decision had been taken that I would not be appointed as Waterstones' MD.

There were a couple of minor issue reasons given, which involved insignificant and easily correctable commercial indicators in the stores over the previous few weeks, and I couldn't understand how this could jeopardise the strategic handover that I thought had been agreed. It was not until later that I understood my own contribution to the issue at the time: I had perceived it as a done deal. I really thought this was *what had been promised*, as it were. As a result, I had been only too happy to listen to the advice to sit back, keep out of trouble and wait for the appointment. This had been my undoing.

What my boss had really wanted to see was me stepping up and into the role – acting up, if you like – immediately. He had a problem with the way the company had been run and in the performance of some departments and directors. I could have stepped in to take some of the slack and provide leadership without the necessity of having the stripes on my shoulders. In his view, I needed to demonstrate that I was capable of doing the job in order to clinch it, but I didn't see that at the time.

There is no guarantee at all that you will be told what to do or what is expected of you. This is a key lesson for aspiring first-time CEOs and MDs, particularly those looking to be appointed as an internal candidate. The elephant in the room is your inexperience as a candidate who does not have experience of running a company as the top person – the leader with the ultimate responsibility for its performance, people and future. Don't wait to be given the keys to show that you can drive.

Being appointed is the easy part

Getting there is clearly not the end of it. I have talked to many successful CEOs who were initially startled by the jump in responsibility and expectation. John Seager, a key figure in the property world in the North East of England, now runs his own successful asset management consultancy. In 2015, he was given a big jump up to his first-time CEO role in a high-profile private/public partnership. This is him on the experience of how he felt at the time and how he looks back at it now:

'I thought: I trust this board, as they recruited me. They know I'm young and inexperienced, so I have some licence to make mistakes. They have my back. Then three of the board immediately resigned and another died. This led to an influx of new board directors and a totally different landscape. My impostor syndrome soared. We had a disaster away-day with a dinner the night before and I wanted to pull the next day with the facilitator, but had to plough on. I was a complete and utter failure. I was deadly serious about going in and saying, "You're paying me too much, I'll take a pay cut." However, the facilitator made it clear that this was not my doing.'

What happened next? John goes on:

'I upped my game massively, controlling the things that I could control. I would rehearse and have the board papers looking spectacular. I presented really well, showing that this place was being run really properly. I began rehearsing the questions that I anticipated they would ask, along with how I was going to respond. I practised out loud how the person who should be doing this job would say this. It had a powerful effect. I remember it dawning on me that I didn't have to defend why they employed me. It also helped me realise I didn't need to be in defensive mode with everything else, either.'

Looking back on this experience, John states how invaluable it has been to his overall development. He now reflects:

> 'That rollercoaster was exactly the right thing for me to prove to myself that I was good at the job. It was better than a fast-track MBA or other academic course – this was real-time, hands-on experience that money can't buy.'

My point is that care and attention in the transition phases here might have prevented a lot of the angst and been more of a guarantee of success. While John rose to the challenge, others may not have. The 'sink or swim when thrown in the deep end' approach is not considered the best strategy these days in identifying or bedding in people into their new roles following promotion. This should be especially so when it is the biggest job in the company.

You can immediately see the difference in approach with an experienced, seasoned and confident leader. Roger Mavity also told me a story of the time he took over as chair of a travel company who had a great reputation with their customers but hadn't made a profit in twenty years. He related that the company's board resented the fact that he had been appointed despite him knowing nothing about the travel industry. Roger pointed out to them that being an expert wasn't much use either, since they were all highly experienced and yet the business continued to lose money. He goes on to explain that it was actually his ignorance in how the industry traditionally worked that allowed him to consider and implement a different way of operating that reversed the company's financial fortune.

There is evidence that CEOs with less experience perform better. Executive recruitment firm Spencer Stuart produced research that first-time CEOs outperformed their more experienced counterparts.[20] Not only that, but 70% of the 855 CEOs included in the research had greater success in their first CEO role compared with their second. Outside of taking on turnarounds as a result of their success, the reasons given support the 'stuck in the tramlines' issues or using methods and processes that had worked for them previously in other companies/industries. Perhaps they tend to focus on cost control and cuts rather than the more difficult, and perhaps less quick, win of driving the top line and delivering growth.

New CEOs tend to be more flexible and adaptable and bring to the position a new lens. A flow-through of new candidates, perhaps including more women and ethnic and socioeconomic minorities, into the top positions is likely to ensure greater diversity rather than recycling the same people around the system.

Keynote takeaway

External confidence is important, but internal confidence is far more difficult to generate. How you use your relationships with others and avoiding isolation is key. You don't need to be hugely experienced to gain confidence and you'll be surprised how others will welcome being included in the deliberation.

FOUR

The CEO Winner's Circle

Unravelling your role as the common thread in all business relationships

'The bonds that unite another person to our self exist only in our mind.'
— Marcel Proust

Daniel Priestley, the highly successful serial entrepreneur whose Dent KPI courses I have attended and enjoyed, recently posted a tweet saying, 'I bumped into a friend who has a corporate job. He was reading a fiction book. It must be absolutely wild to have that level of certainty.'[21] His point was about the level of underlying uncertainty entrepreneurs face compared to people who have 'secure jobs' and can switch off more easily. However, there's perhaps an inference that business people should have their heads buried in a business book or be listening to a billionaire genius' podcast rather than wasting their time on fiction. I did take him up on this, as I am a strong believer in the proven value of reading fiction in enhancing the theory of mind, critical thinking and empathy in its readers. Think of it as exercise for the brain, using muscles that are not used every day.

I recently finished *Birnam Wood*,[22] the latest novel by Booker Prize-winning New Zealand author Eleanor Catton, which is an eco-thriller described in *The Guardian* as 'hippies v billionaires'.[23] One piece of dialogue in it struck me as very relevant to first-time CEOs, and I incorporate this thinking into my coaching with them:

> 'What if we stopped talking in terms of individuals at all, and instead we took the relationship as the basis of the socio-economic unit? The relationship, the bonds, the connections – they're just as basic to any system as the actual individuals, the actual data. Right? And in relationships, we do all sorts of things that radically challenge the neoliberal status quo: we make sacrifices, we put the other person first, we learn to compromise, we care, we help, we listen, we give ourselves away – and fundamentally, those are different kinds of sacrifices to the kind that are all about self-discipline and following a regime.'

I have been tapped on the shoulder for the majority of my jobs and promotions, and I have been trusted to create a valuable contribution to the company when given a new role. It's clear to me that the most important factor in your business career is how you manage the key relationships that you have. This chapter takes a deeper look at the relationships that you will need to develop and master.

The vital relationships and transition

The job is not done when the new CEO has been chosen and signed up – it's just beginning. The failure rates of between one third and one half are testament to this, and politics and relationships are the biggest contributors to their downfall. The actual transition into the role is often underestimated in a way that would not happen with more junior roles. It's just as important to prepare the direct reports and the company for a new CEO's arrival. The biggest job in the world is arguably President of the United States. There is nearly a three-month gap between the declaration of the election's winner to the inauguration day when they take up office, and a transition team is appointed to help manage the process. The role of the outgoing incumbent can also play an important part in any takeover. The difference between a smooth process and one distorted by attempts to cling on to power and drive insurrection was clearly illustrated in the US Presidential interregnum of 2020/2021.[24]

In my company, Grey Area Coaching, I have devised an eight-stage process that I use for first-time CEOs. It's called the CEO Winner's Circle and it addresses all the key relationships that leaders need to develop and get right in order to be successful. These include critical relationships both inside and outside the company.

The interesting thing about these critical relationships is that every individual is different and there's no set answer that can be applied in all cases to any category. Any great sports athlete who competes against others will be trained to make initial moves or set plays to defeat an opponent, but the truly great individuals and teams transcend that and *play what is in front of them*. They play with their heads up, assessing what the opposition is doing. They override the set play that the hours of practice have tried to instil as second nature and just go for it: the drop shot in tennis, the sidestep and outside break in rugby or, most obviously, the strategy and reaction on a chess board. Set plays will only get you so far – and remember, those on the other side will have done their homework; they will know what you are likely to do in any given circumstance and will have a plan in place to counter it. As Mike Tyson famously said in answer to the question about whether he was concerned about his next opponent's strategy to defeat him: 'Everyone has a plan until they get hit.' This is widely misquoted as '...until they are punched in the mouth/face,' but you get the point.

What is less widely reported is how he continued with: 'Then, like a rat, they stop in fear and freeze.'[25] My take on work relationships is not based on threats, or actual violence, or inspiring frozen fear in others; I've experienced it in the past but it's old-school and no longer valid. If you have been trained as a psychologist, you'll know that the power of leading and positivity is stronger and longer lasting than frightening others to bend them to your will. Emotional intelligence is the new assertiveness.

That apart, arguably there is no right or wrong answer in any given situation in a relationship, as the person opposite you may react differently to the person before or the next person – their reaction may, indeed, be unique. There are likelihoods, certainly, but no certainty.

New CEOs can be prepared for what they need to do, but are most often unprepared for the psychological and emotional intricacies and impacts associated with the role. This is why coaching, mentoring and business books all handle this critical area of relationships differently. Business books tend to follow a format of the top five things to do/avoid to succeed and that's very difficult to do with relationships. There are no bullet points on exactly what to do when you don't know exactly what is going on in the head of the person opposite you or how they will react to something. *'If x happens, then do y'* works less well here. That's why I like to provide coaching and mentoring support to first-time CEOs, and why I prefer to work one-to-one with them. We need to explore feelings and reactions, being able to read the signals from the other person, and how to react – how to play what is in front of us.

The Myers-Briggs Type Indicator was developed in the middle of the last century and was an attempt to categorise people into different basic types based on their answers to a questionnaire.[26] In the late 1980s, it was developed into a scoring system and was widely used by the 'personnel departments', as they were then known, to assist in recruitment, training and development. At its most basic, it assigned levels of extraversion and introversion according to the preferences indicated by answers to the questions. Such theories as this have lost much of their credibility and are sometimes categorised as pseudoscience with little actual merit. I have heard Myers-Briggs described as 'astrology for business' and can see something in that.

What they *do* offer is the confirmation that there are many different types of people out there, and how you treat or react to them is going to be taken differently by each type, and to a certain extent, every individual. It also promotes the thought that there is a place for everyone, and a high-performing team will likely benefit from the balance that diverse representation can provide. Wildly positive extroverts can irritate and actually demotivate others, but in their early working years may find it difficult to understand this effect and others' reactions. There's a difference between being thoughtful and being a negative-energy sponge that consigns everything to the 'No' bin automatically.

Every good leader knows to do two things when hiring their team. First, they should hire the best possible people – ideally people who are better than themselves. If the CEO is the ultimate general manager, they may need highly specialised people in specialist positions and they need to consider their general management skills, or at least potential, as far as managing their teams and succession planning goes. The poor leader worries that hiring very talented people as their direct reports means they are recruiting a threat to their own position. The good leader understands that hiring the most talented team possible will lead to the best results for the company, and that this is the ultimate measure of their own success.

Second, they should hire people who bring other characteristics rather than hiring in their own likeness. A representative balance needs to be achieved. If we all were natural risk takers and thought it was worth a go to dive into the sea off a cliff even if there was only a 40% chance of survival, then we wouldn't last long. We need, and should welcome, challenge in order to make the best decisions. The ultimate call is with the CEO, and being a leader means being able to make those calls, but the quality of the decisions made will improve if they have been examined and considered from different angles.

The CEO Winner's Circle

As the CEO Winner's Circle identifies, there are many different levels of relationship to get right. In addition to two out of five new CEOs failing, research found that 82% of those new CEOs fail because they don't build relationships with their people.[27]

The CEO Winner's Circle examines the relationships that first-time CEOs need to get right in order to be successful

I am a passionate believer that every first-time CEO should have a professional, independent coach/mentor assigned to them. It makes complete financial sense to underpin the new CEO with the best support possible in order to boost their chance of success.

The decisions that a CEO takes can account for over 40% of the performance by the company. It has also been reported that when CEOs fail, their direct reports' performance drops by 15% and the danger of them leaving rises by 20%.[28] This is before the resulting cost of the recruitment process of any replacements, induction and delay in getting up to speed.

The CEO Winner's Circle starts with *you*. It also continues and ends with *you*, as you are the one consistent piece in all the relationships that you have as a first-time CEO. As a result, it's the most important piece, and it starts before anyone else is involved. How you perceive yourself and the thoughts that you bring to the table are incredibly important and influential, as the first three chapters in this book have spelled out. This is where a coach/mentor can help you to develop yourself and bring your 'A game' to the table every time.

The rest of this book will examine how you lead, manage, delegate, interact and communicate with the other areas identified within the CEO Winner's Circle.

Managing upwards will look at the relationships with your board, investors and stakeholders – your bosses, in effect. These may include the chair and/or key shareholders. This can be an area that leads to a lot of personal stress and is vital to not only your and the company's performance, but also to your wellbeing and life. In one way, it's arguably the most important of the relationships as they probably were involved in giving you the job in the first place and have the power to change their minds. Having a positive relationship here – one as equals – makes a dramatic difference to how you feel about your own role.

Direct Reports are the meat and drink of your daily working life relationships. This is the group that you work most closely with to run the business. This is the 'first team', and you are the captain. If this team has been selected wisely, works well together and contains individuals who can be trusted to run their own teams effectively, then there is little you cannot achieve. There is no 'one size fits all' approach on how to do this, and every member of the team will need their own bespoke approach from you to bring out their best. There is real skill in getting this right. Many CEOs will look critically at individual members of their exec team when perhaps the first aspect they should be examining is their own methods of trying to get the best out of them.

Becoming known as a leader that is great to work for and who develops people will also improve your ability to attract that best talent to work with you.

Then there is the wider company. This includes every single individual on the company payroll. You are now responsible for their livelihood and how you run the company will affect not only their lives but those of their families and dependants. You may have been less interested in some sides of the business in the past or you may have even found some boring and dull. That stops immediately you are appointed as CEO – in fact, it stops long before you wish to be considered as a CEO. Any good board director will understand the contribution by their fellow directors and their respective functions. This is the conductor and the orchestra, bringing out the best of each section to create the most harmonious and impressive whole. The triangle in the timpani section is as vital as the brass, and the flute needs to be heard alongside the kettle drums. All eyes are on the leader, and they take their cues from their leader.

Next, we look outside the company. First at our clients, suppliers and partners. This includes partners in the supply chain as well as agencies and freelancers who make up a wider team that we rely on to be a successful business. Just because they aren't on our regular payroll doesn't mean that they aren't a critical contributor to what we do. The quality of their input will rise or fall depending on our relationship with them. How we treat them, how we include them and how we react to each other will play an important part in getting the best out of these relationships.

We will also look at the wider industry and how the first-time CEO sits in the bigger picture and their standing within it. These may be within trade associations, or their role in innovation, efficiencies or environmental sustainability for their particular trade. Doing things for the good of the whole industry rather than just for their own company.

Here also there is the relationship with the media, whether that is with the trade publishing magazines or with national media, when applicable. Your standing will contribute to whether people want to come and work for your company. How you are perceived and perform will likely have a direct relationship with how your company is perceived and performs. It will also be influenced by your relationship with the media and this can be managed much like any other.

The CEO Winner's Circle process

The CEO Winner's Circle process is designed to get you from where you are now to where you want to be.[29] The process helps you identify what obstacles have been preventing you getting there and provides a bridge to help you get past them.

We'll then review what we have learned, as how we handle success has important lessons too. Celebrating success with your team is valuable, but crowing about it is a very different thing.

In my family we are highly competitive and enjoy playing games. We often play 'Spoof' (the three-coin counting/gambling game) to decide who needs to do something – generally a task that you'd rather not do, given the choice. The most important regulation is the 'Gloating Rule' that comes automatically into effect. If one person wins by choosing the correct total amount of coins in a round, and then reacts to this with a big 'Yeeeessss!' and a fist-pump, then they have their win negated for gloating and they're back in the game. It's a very popular rule for all but one player when applied.

In business, revelling in your own success is not a great look, particularly from the view of others who have lost as a result. Celebration of negotiation successes or similar, where you big up your own win and diminish that of the vanquished, rarely goes down well. It's a small world, and each industry is smaller still; karma has a way of finding out those who beat their chests too overtly while standing over their conquest. It's never wise to burn your bridges as you never know who your next boss may turn out to be.

Finally, we'll look at how you keep positive and moving forward with your career. A quarterly health check – an MOT on your business attitude and attributes, if you like – can be invaluable in ensuring that nothing slips and that any new inputs, people, variables, or situations are not starting to create a block. Coaching and mentoring benefits everyone. No matter how experienced, senior or successful you become, the ability to detect and solve your own problems is immeasurably harder than doing it for others. If Bill Gates can still benefit from executive coaching, the rest of us probably can too.[30]

Keynote takeaway

Relationships need work, building, care and attention just as much as any project, and generally more. They are inconsistent and they change based on circumstances that can be out of your control. But they are the key that will unlock amazing potential that will surprise everyone involved. Investing time into the crucial relationships always pays off.

PART TWO
INTERNAL RELATIONSHIPS

FIVE

CEO Gymnastics

Managing upwards with grace and balance

'I like not only to be loved, but also to be told
I am loved.'
— George Eliot

When I was appointed to the board of HMV, I didn't realise that I had done the hard part by having been selected by the MD for the role – I knew I had to go and be interviewed by the chairman of the group too. As with all interview preparation, I mentally and orally rehearsed (always include practising out loud) what I would bring to the role, why I was the right person to do the job, where I believed the company needed to go and how I could help it get there. I also assembled some considered questions to ask that would show insight, curiosity and nous. The interview went like this:

CHAIR: 'So, where do you think HMV
is heading?'

ME: 'Well, I'd really like to hear your strategic
view of where you would like to take it…'

An hour later, I had not said much more, but the chair was delighted that it had gone so satisfactorily and that we both were in agreement that his vision for the company was the right one and all would be well. Potentially the biggest interview of my life to date had also been the easiest.

Relationships with your bosses are critical and will determine how far you get in your career. In the case of the interview above, floating downstream with the direction of flow was the right thing to do. Now that I had the position, I had the chance to prove myself by my performance within the role. Job done for the time being. If I had followed the same plan with the MD in my attempt to secure this board position of product director, then it would have been a disaster. The close relationship that we had needed to be supported by belief on both sides that I could not only deliver in this newly created role but could also grow both it and my department to leverage our market position as number one with our suppliers – the record and film companies. This would put the company in a position to support our stores with buying and range control so that the store base could expand at a much faster rate than before, as it was quicker to obtain the sites and build the stores than it was to develop the experienced store managers who could run their stores both autonomously and successfully.

As it had not been done before in our company, we had to believe in the plan. But the company also needed to be able to flex, adapt, grow and flex depending on markets and change. The introduction of DVD as a replacement for VHS was one such seismic transformation and the emergence of video games as a force was another. I could not prove via my career to date that I had the experience of doing all these things, but I had demonstrated the ability to take on important new projects and not only learn and grow in the role, but lead the company to success when doing so. It was the attributes that I had demonstrated that put me in the position of being considered the best candidate for the job. Gave me the luck, if you like.

Trying to second-guess what it is that your boss wants you to say and attempting to fill the gap accordingly will prove to be problematic. This is not the way to build the relationship in a credible, lasting and positive manner. The expression 'managing upwards' is used to impart that you need to affect control of that connection in the same way as you would with those reporting into you.

Understanding what you both want and need from the relationship

The critical point is to have an honest understanding, and agreement, of where you need support and how you discuss issues as equals.

The term 'delegating upwards' implies that you have needs and requests for your boss to provide if you are to deliver your goals. This is often less understood.

My first board director position was a success but was not without its hiccoughs and provided me with an excellent lesson in managing upwards. I had been on the board for a couple of years and the company, department and I were performing well – or so I thought. At one quarterly review where we re-forecasted the business, I was given the task of renegotiating our file terms with record companies specialising in 12" dance singles to be more reflective of our growing market share in this department. This was October, and in November I needed to concentrate on the DVD launch that was happening across the UK.

This sexy new format was going to take over from VHS, and homes across the UK would be transformed from shelves full of bulky stashes of VHS by couch potatoes into shiny film and cultural collections that show off families as fans of the creative arts. The problem was the film companies wanted to use this opportunity to change the way pricing was structured to benefit the suppliers and penalise the retailers. To cut a long story short, I led the fight back, prevented this happening, struck a unique, first-mover partnership with Warner Brothers (who were spearheading the launch) and, overnight, positioned us as the market share leader in home entertainment on DVD from having been number two on video. A good month's work I thought.

My next forecast meeting with the MD reflected this deal, which would make HMV millions over the next few years. It also showed I had made little headway renegotiating with the dance record companies, but that was small beer and most of their people weren't around in December. My boss at the time was incandescent about this and refused to acknowledge the groundbreaking DVD deal by way of an explanation, likening it to our 'finance director paying an invoice'. This led to a letter being sent to me which I still have to this day. It said that my performance was unacceptable, was not at the required level and that I would be micromanaged with immediate effect. Should things not improve considerably in the next few weeks, I would be sacked.

I was shocked – particularly as I thought I had pulled off the deal of the decade at the time for the company. I had to decide how to react to this setback.

Fast forward a few months and I'm giving a keynote address at the annual store managers' conference.

I have always enjoyed writing and mostly get a kick from delivering speeches, and this one had gone down pretty well. I remember my boss and the HR director at the time congratulating me, saying that not many people bounce back the way that I had from where I was a few months ago. Most people sink, but I'd reacted brilliantly. 'You were on fire today!' they exclaimed.

Readers, what had I done differently to turn things around? In my business performance and how I went about things: nothing. In the way I managed the relationship with my boss: total transformation. I provided routine and regular information, set out what I aimed to achieve and reported against it and presented options when appropriate and sought advice. I also kept communication flowing regularly – a vacuum is an incubator for suspicion, conspiracy theories and incorrect assumptions. These were incredibly important lessons, and they are generic. How you play them with each individual boss will differ.

The transition is rarely planned sufficiently for you

I discussed earlier the lack of preparation that often accompanies the appointment of a new CEO – that the hard part has been done and the new incumbent will hit the ground running once they start. The failure rate of new CEOs is testament to this being a reality, and the blame for this has to lie heavily with the chair and the board that make the appointment. What can the incoming CEO do about this?

If you are a first-time CEO, it's not easy. The inexperience of knowing what you need, coupled with the weight of impostor syndrome, make a conversation about your foibles and concerns a difficult one to initiate. However, if there is a review of cultural and personal factors that need to be addressed alongside the business goals and KPIs, then this will help normalise these aspects rather than burying them. That's assuming that these have been identified in the first place – not all companies have a good antenna on these softer scenarios, yet we have seen it's these relationships that can be the downfall of new CEOs.

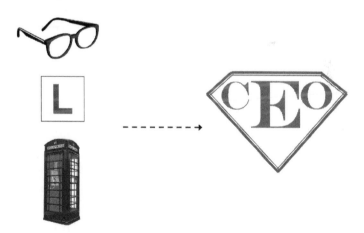

The transition to become a successful CEO
needs to be planned and supported

And there's the (potential) impostor syndrome that needs to be addressed. As well as providing an independent coach/mentor to help, one idea given to me by John Seager was that every first-time CEO should be provided with a one-pager statement from the board that lays out why they employed them: the achievements that impressed them and why that individual is best suited for the role. For someone suffering from hidden self-esteem issues, this would provide a regular reminder of why they are the right person for the job.

Managing the board

The board will hopefully be made up with experienced and sometimes brilliant people. Martyn Gibbs, the former CEO of Game Digital, was kind enough to write the foreword to this book. He reflected, 'The sheer intellectual powerhouses you can be dealing with are undoubtedly a significant move on from anything experienced before.' This may also be the case among the investors you are introduced to.

The relationship with board directors is one that can be difficult to position correctly. If the directors lean in too close, this could be taken as a lack of trust – distance themselves too far, and it means that you are thrown in the deep end and are on your own. In a 2012 survey conducted by RHR International, 57% of internally promoted CEOs and 87% of external appointments defined their board as being 'less involved' than they believe they should have been to optimise their success.[31] The happier the board are with their appointment, perhaps the less they believe the new CEO will need, or indeed want, their involvement outside board meetings. Looking confident and in control is no indicator of how you are coping internally. It is important to get to know each of the directors as individuals.

The relationship with the chair is the most important of all the board directors, obviously. Some CEOs have very positive, strong relationships with their chair, with clear delineation of accountability. It may be that good friendships develop between them and it's ideal not to worry about what they are thinking, to build trust and be able to lean on them at times, perhaps around investor issues or just on general topics when required. This is the type of relationship that CEOs should strive to achieve.

There is also a difference between executive chairs and non-executive chairs. In the case of private equity owned companies, it can be common for one individual to be chair of multiple companies to keep a close eye and protect their investment. This can make it difficult to get the time to build that relationship.

At one point in my time as CEO at Borders, I had such a chair. Our head office was above our Charing Cross Road store in London's West End and I got a call one day from our chair who was in the shop below. He started ranting and remonstrating loudly on the phone, so I went down to see what the matter was. It was somewhat dark in the store and he immediately berated me for this, saying the lightbulbs had been allowed to go out without being replaced and cussing in front of all and sundry that this was basic retail standards stuff, calling us all useless and turning on his tail and stomping out of the store. I then went to the counter and asked the rather shocked assistant manager if we had experienced a power cut, which, of course, we had. I rang the chair and explained this to him, and he grudgingly agreed to go for a coffee.

'It's important that we get on,' I said.

'No, it isn't,' he replied. 'I'd work with the Devil if they made me a profit.' There are some people who are easier to work with than others. Motivating people to perform at their best and openly declaring using 'fear of the sack' as your incentive of choice – very common in my time climbing up the greasy pole – is now seen as rather old-school and ineffective in getting the best results over time.

I said earlier that second-guessing what your boss wants you to say is not what should be done. Getting a full understanding of how they like information and proposals to be structured and how much information to provide upfront is a very valid piece of research. Having individual conversations with board members to establish their favoured modus operandi is extremely helpful. And vice versa: how can the board help and how do they foster a positive atmosphere at board meetings and one-to-ones? The individual relationships with directors outside of the collective board meetings is critical to establish allies and lobbying lines to enable productive board meetings.

Succession – the script for success

If your company takes CEO succession seriously, they need to have a leadership development programme that dovetails with a board and CEO succession plan.

This needs to be given time, attention and priority by the board, and this results in the new CEO already having relationships with board members. However, this is closer to being the exception rather than the rule. Given what has been said about the importance of the CEO for company performance, the high rate of failure and the cost of getting it wrong, this is a surprisingly perennial problem.

The lack of a succession plan means that CEOs are more likely to be selected from external candidates. The board looks for someone who ideally has a track record that demonstrates they can do the job. The track record of success for external appointments is that they get binned more often than internal candidates.[32] The missing piece tends to be around fit, culture, relationships and the ability to listen and communicate. Somewhere among the relationships that are critical to both their success and survival, there is a disconnect which is exposed and creates the hole in the net that is supporting them.

Of course, internal candidates may bring the disadvantage of being too close and not being able to see the bigger picture with new eyes in a way that an external appointment might. They may be the continuity appointment at a time when this is not what is needed. In this day and age, when change is the new normal, this can be a danger.

In both cases, it's critical that the attitude and approach of the candidates, and the emotional intelligence and ability to recruit and lead teams and the company is taken into strong consideration as well as the KPI achievements on the CV.

What can the new CEO do, other than building direct relationships with the individual board members and the chair?

It is important to get involved with the building blocks of planning at the earliest time for the direction of travel to be agreed and major U-turns or roadblocks to be avoided.

When I was running Borders, we had managed a turnaround, achieving six quarters of like-for-like growth in a difficult market and were starting to generate a consistent profit even though we were in expansion mode. Our US Group Company then announced overnight that they were 'exploring strategic alternatives' for all their international operations – ie, we were up for sale, along with our counterparts outside the USA. In the UK, Merrill Lynch was appointed to run the process, with Ernst & Young managing the data room. We produced our information memorandum and had a fair few companies poring over the numbers – including all our competitors, I'm sure.

When it became clear to me who was going to buy us, I went into more detail with them about my plan for the future of the company under new owners. Not just the what we were going to need to do, but also getting into the how we were going to do it. There needed to be a separation from the US company and systems and there was going to be a guillotine that would come down on a certain date, which dictated a very tight rollout schedule for implementing replacement systems. This meant the tills in the stores, the accounting systems that ran the business and the stock management systems that managed the range of hundreds of thousands of different lines. As a result, we had already hammered out our specification, run our beauty parade to assess a variety of options, selected the best and most cost-effective solution, had developers, fitters and trainers ready to go and had the hardware and software identified and allocated ready to ship according to our defined schedule. The whole thing was planned as far as it could be without spending a penny, and ready to go as soon as the new owner was in position and put their signature on the cheque.

Clearly, it was vital to ensure that as much pre-planning work and agreement was in place prior to the sale formalities being completed by the lawyers and accountants. The decision to proceed could be agreed even if the green light had not been given. This was sensible, pragmatic and pre-empting in the best way and meant that on the day the purchase of the company went through, the Capex request form could be signed by the new owner and the project would move into action.

What I didn't expect, given this pre-work, was the complete change of mindset from the new owner/chair when it came to signing on the dotted line. He had been to a dinner party recently and mentioned Borders needing new systems and someone else had said there were cheaper options he could consider than the one we had meticulously chosen. Despite the months of precision specification and selection by our team, the pressing deadline that had now been set, and taking him through the results of this process in detail in advance, he had a last-minute change of mind. He told me he had been involved with new systems at Whittard of Chelsea, the coffee and tea retailers that handle hundreds of centrally ordered lines, so had a good idea of what was required. I responded that I had project managed the entire systems implementation at both HMV and Waterstones which carried hundreds of thousands of lines with a database of millions more to select from, and a complex balance of central and store ordering – exactly the situation that Borders faced.

In this instance, I was overruled, and a new consultant was to be appointed to redo the whole exercise. This was followed in short order by a similar overruling decision on the recommendation from the CFO and me for an entire shortlist for the bank we should use, and also a U-turn to retain an exec team member despite a fantastic replacement already being offered their job.

Establish where you draw your own line

There are times when you have to make a hard decision. You have pushed back but it makes no difference. Are you prepared to 'run' a company according to the game plan that someone else presents you with? Even if you put together the plan and involve the chair in the signoff process along the way, are you prepared to accept last-minute dictatorial changes with little or no rationale or connection with the work put in to date or the experience or knowledge from those who have been steeped in this industry or business? The answer for me was no. I knew that many incumbent CEOs don't survive a takeover and I was not prepared to push water uphill or merely carry out orders from someone who I didn't believe had the long-term interests of the company at heart. I left the company and the job that I had most enjoyed. Among my chair's last words to me were, 'You'll be surprised how quickly the water closes over your head.' As someone once said to me, 'It's all part of life's rich patisserie…'.

As it turned out, the new systems consultant recommended the product of their sister company, and the Icelandic bank that my CFO and I identified as the one not to touch with a bargepole was chosen and failed within a few months. The private equity company sold Borders less than two years later to a management buyout backed by a company with a reputation at the time for asset-stripping and it went bust shortly after. I felt extremely sorry for the staff, but I am very glad that I left when I did and would not have wished to be at the helm when the ship went under, particularly as I was witnessing what I saw as the wrong decisions being taken from the off.

Now, many years later, I am an experienced chair and I look back from a different position and try and see how I might have played things differently at the time as a CEO. The result I see is that the honest answer is the right card, and how and when to play it is the game. I would have changed a few things, of course, but nothing dramatically. My view on the chairs and bosses that I have had has changed little, but I would have played my hand rather differently on many occasions. For example, when considering risk-taking, I would have gone for the more risky, bigger win option more often in the knowledge that if I failed, at least I failed attempting something ambitious and big. To have opted for the easier route and failed at that would, indeed, have been a disaster.

One saying that I would have acted on from the off is, 'What you allow is what will continue'. Challenging and shutting down any unacceptable and bullying behaviour as soon as it surfaces is essential in creating a positive and constructive place to work. I've been called out on it myself on occasions when stressed and rectified poor behaviour as a result. As Sheryl Sandberg, the COO of Facebook, said, 'So please ask yourself: What would I do if I weren't afraid? And then go do it.'[33] That's the type of relationships and conditions that encourage great performance.

Keynote takeaway

Managing upwards successfully unlocks resources and experience you need to do your job effectively and makes your life easier in general. The transition and approach require a bespoke style based on the individual characters and relationships, and needs time, knowledge, attention and thought on what each expects.

SIX

Herding Unicorns

The first-time CEO's playbook for managing direct reports with magic and mastery

'The first method for estimating the intelligence of a ruler is to look at the men he has around him.'
— Niccolo Machiavelli

S tephen Bayley, design guru and co-author of, among many others, the book *Life's a Pitch: How to sell yourself and your brilliant ideas,*[34] told me the following:

'I like the old Zen saying that whatever is true, the opposite is truer. This allows me, very conveniently, to accommodate contrary beliefs at the same time. So, I am certain that in an organisation you can achieve anything, provided you don't want to take the credit. Alternatively, employ the best people and

take credit for their achievements yourself.
Each is possibly correct. But frankly, I think
the only route to enduring success is to have
immaculate taste and to Hell with the rest
of them.'

I think there is a spot of poetic licence here, or creative eccentricity perhaps, rather than advice to be taken seriously. But there is a point in that it re-emphasises that it is you who are at the centre of these relationships and you can control them in different ways. I recently had a coaching call from a CEO who wished to discuss taking me on to provide some coaching to the joint MDs who ran one of her companies. The more she explained about their situations and what she wanted the outcomes to be, the clearer it was to me that it was her who needed the coaching in order to establish what her own longer-term goals were and clarify how the different strands were involved; how they needed to be worked on and aligned so that they all led in that direction could then follow.

The relationship with your direct reports is probably the most crucial of all. The Senior Leadership or Executive Team (SLT) is the group running the business every day. Their responsibilities tend to be functional at the director level – Operations, Finance, Sales, etc – but it's the CEO who needs to concentrate on the overall bigger picture and make sure that the component parts are fitting together to make the whole flourish. The CEO is the orchestra conductor

I mentioned earlier, or the chef who pulls the ingredients together to make the meal – it's an art as much as a science, and presentation is important.

The dynamics in this group are critical and the individual relationships with the CEO will vary. Some individuals may feel that they should have been appointed to the CEO role themselves and may feel aggrieved, and even reluctant, to help the new CEO succeed. If the appointment was internal, the new CEO was their peer up until they were elevated to the role, and the relationship balance changes immediately.

For the CEO, this can be dramatic. From being one of several working as a team, they are suddenly given the ultimate responsibility and need to ensure that their directors deliver. It's a big transition and it's lonely at the top. The appointment may give them the authority in the form of title and reporting lines, but it doesn't necessarily provide them with the tools, experience or support to take over effectively from day one. The previous chapter covered this lack of preparation.

The expectations of you and your expectations of others

People also treat you differently. Discussing this with his colleagues at Deloitte, Director Dan Oakey told me the following:

'As CEO, all of a sudden, nobody laughs at your jokes anymore. You have become the target of their comedy. Not everybody wishes you well. It's easy to believe in meritocracy when you're the one who has risen to the top, but other people have motives to believe very different things.'

As someone who enjoys the team element, this struck me when I was appointed. People look at you differently, as if you should know the answer to everything. You need to make it clear that, on the contrary, you have the questions to everything now. Asking the best question is what sets you apart.

For external appointments, even for first-time CEOs, the assumption is generally that they come pre-loaded with all the experience, answers, talent and ability to plug and play into the company and start delivering better results immediately and a long-term strategy that will improve everything. Any lack of confidence will probably be hidden and the brave face will likely not look like it is an invitation to provide help. The default is *leave them to get on with it*. This can create a vicious circle which compounds any impostor syndrome experienced. It is not impostor syndrome to examine and identify what your weak spots are. They are likely to get exposed, so plan for it, improve, delegate and manage it.

Delegation is a key word here. Up until now, you have been responsible for an area, a division, or perhaps a function in which you have specialised. You were responsible for it delivering or exceeding the budgeted results. As CEO, you are now responsible for the total company performance, but in a way, you can't really run the company. Everyone who reports to you has their area of responsibility which aggregate to make up the company performance.

The director that the rest of the board have sympathy for tends to be the one that is in charge of the area that the CEO has come from. If the CEO is an internal appointment, they may even be the CEO's successor in that position. Delegating to people running areas that you believe them to be an expert in, and in which you have familiarity but not expertise, is doable. Delegating to someone with less experience than you in an area that you are an expert in is far more difficult.

This can also flip. Leticia Rita is CEO of a company called HolaBrief, who provide an online tool for agency owners to collaborate with their clients successfully. She told me an interesting story about her experience of delegation:

> I had a problem with delegation – nobody could do things as well as I could, and it was quicker to do it myself than explain what was required. Of course, I didn't have the time to do everything, so this was unsustainable.

Then we hired a product manager who changed the world – she was on the same wavelength and just got it. She was super-talented, so we gave her more to do. Then we started giving her everything. Six months later she was burned out, and the best employee we had ever had left the company. She hadn't complained and we hadn't checked in. The lesson learned was that it's my responsibility to find out how people are coping rather than theirs to tell me if they're not. Also, not to let things get to breaking point before reining it back – that option may not be available anymore.'

This is an excellent lesson to learn, albeit the hard way. You will probably spend the initial part of your induction/transition listening to people at all levels in your company and, in particular, your direct reports. At some point you will have garnered enough answers to your questions to form an opinion about their capability, their abilities and their competence. What you may not know about is their current situation and whether that reflects accurately what their capacity and potential are at the moment.

There are bosses whose automatic, go-to response to a decline in performance or missing the numbers will be to give a bollocking and double down with threats of what might happen if the results don't pick up. At one stage, I knew that I was going to be handing in my notice at a company imminently and, therefore, also secretly knew that a particular meeting with the MD and all the regional managers would be my last one there. At that gathering, the MD berated the regional managers for their recent sales performance and actually used the phrase 'fear of the sack' as his motivational tool. I sat there with a poker face, inwardly delighted that this would be my last such meeting and determined that I would do whatever I could in my career to move the dial to a more positive and inspirational position. The constant use of the whip is just so old-school and unacceptable. Not only is it ineffective in achieving the desired result over time, but it can end wonderful careers where a performance dip may well be temporary, and for reasons completely beyond work. I wish I had stood up to such practice earlier and more frequently in my career.

Getting to the root of the problem

It is dangerous to assume that performance is solely an attitude issue that can be rectified by a boot up the arse. Are you the kind of boss that someone could come to and explain that they're acting as end-of-life carer to their aged father with Parkinson's disease, having recently moved him into a home after he was widowed last year? Do you even know what it takes to be that kind of boss? And even if it is a work issue that's driving underperformance, it could be something specific that is blocking your staff that they can't resolve on their own. Any coach knows that by asking the right questions, you can unlock massive latent potential in all kinds of different people and teams.

It's only by understanding your direct reports thoroughly that you can answer the most important delegation question: just how much rope do you give each of them? It certainly won't be the same for everyone around the table, and the amount given out will change for each individual over time. Hopefully this becomes greater as experience grows and, alongside it, trust, but sometimes it may be less if things need closer assessment. This doesn't mean robotically slapping a warning on the individual and insisting on a declared, micro-performance-management process. It can be as subtle as declaring a particular interest in an area and asking to be involved more closely in meetings or reviews to familiarise yourself or provide specialist support.

The current, post-pandemic restabilising of office attendance versus working from home and finding the right balance is an interesting area here. Clearly there are pros and cons both ways, with potentially significant time savings from not commuting alongside potential cost-saving too. Also, the ability to work in a less interrupted and focused environment, particularly if the tasks you do require detailed attention – editors in publishing allegedly respond well to this for their meticulous work. On the office side is the ability to work in teams, particularly creatively, or to absorb the culture and pick up learning osmotically from those around you, especially when nearer the beginning of your time at a company.

What has shifted is the culture of suspicion that surrounded working from home ('WFH') prior to the pandemic. The assumption that people would slack unless they were under your nose, and you could keep a good eye on them is not the motivational nirvana that we should be aspiring to. When moving companies, I learned the difference between issuing JFDI orders (Just F***ing Do It) to get things done versus taking the time to explain the rationale and shared beneficial outcome that meant we were all motivated to hit the target. There is no reason why your team should not be effective for the periods when they are working from home. It was many years ago that Henry Ford, founder of the Ford Motor Company, said, 'Quality means doing it right when no one is looking.'[35]

In one way, measuring people by their results is easier and has more clarity when people work remotely. It's the only measure that you may have, and retailers understand this, as members of a London head office are unlikely to visit their outpost in Inverness each month. I learned to delegate relatively early, possibly because I was concerned that my general management skills meant I had few specialist skills, so I had no choice. The important thing was to agree the desired outcome, responsibility and timing. How it was done was down to the individual, and we could revisit the resources required, etc, as the method became established. I was, however, a stickler for monthly reports for use at our board meetings and one-to-ones to review progress against the agreed goal. I think this was part of the project manager in me that knew others might be knocked sideways if their dependencies were not met and the overall critical path would suffer as a result.

I remember one director who delighted in the freedom that I gave them to deliver but hated having to write a report every month. They couldn't reconcile the two things and said, 'You seem so relaxed about delegating and such a pain in the neck about reporting – I just don't understand where you're coming from?' I had to explain to them that it was the reporting – the knowing how it was going, whether it was on track, and whether I needed to dive in deeper – that allowed me to give them the freedom to carry on as they saw fit. This seemed obvious to me but not so to all of my reports.

Creating a talented and balanced team

It also seems obvious that the CEO should surround themselves with the best talent possible. I am only emphasising that you need to forget concerns that you may be hiring someone who may end up challenging you for your job. You want the company to do as well as possible and your functional heads, the senior leadership team, to be the best it can be. Your job is not only to help them individually do the best job that they can, but you also need to knot the team together so that they perform and integrate well collectively.

If you can go on holiday for two weeks (or more) and the business hums on fantastically while you are away, it doesn't mean you are not needed – it means the opposite: you are fantastic at your job.

God, I'm good

The team balance needs to be considered when recruiting, and it needs to happen whenever the team meets – be that SLT meetings, board meetings, or more occasional set pieces such as awaydays. Recruitment so often revolves around the most difficult criterion to measure: the *fit*. Will they fit into this organisation? Will they get what we are about? Will those in the company respond well to them? This has validity, yes, but it can also be an excuse, sometimes subconsciously, to hire in your own likeness and create an echo chamber rather than an environment of diversity of thought and constructive challenge.

There is a consistent call for diversity but it's more than the representation in a photograph around the boardroom table. It requires the representatives having different opinions and life-experiences as well. There has to be challenge and disagreement, and even dispute, to prove that the policy is working. If you look at the current, tired Conservative Government as I write in the summer of 2023, this looks like an administration that has run out of steam. On paper, it's the most diverse set of ministers on record and includes the first British Asian and Hindu to become Prime Minister. In practice, it seems to be a collection of head-nodders who provide little challenge to the top and see no need to deviate from a relentless path to placate the far-right of their party.

Awaydays and team building are fun and motivational to some and the worst nightmare to others. The idea of abseiling down a cliff is not for me and I know from experience that a day West African drumming (listen, trust, coordinate, communicate, create, develop, adapt, etc) is worse than purgatory for others. A day designed to help create a team can also confirm just how broken it is at the time. The awaydays that I have been to and that have really worked well have always been a success because of a fantastic facilitator. An independent professional who is accomplished at bringing issues out and ensuring that everyone is both involved and enthused. This is a real skill, and a lot more difficult than handing out some Lego and giving you two minutes to build something that represents the hope for the future to you. When done brilliantly, facilitation can also seem like magic and works particularly well for more disparate groups who meet occasionally, such as boards of trustees.

There is a lot of stuff that we could talk about here, but if we get on to Vision and Mission Statements then all could be lost, and we will never emerge from that rabbit hole. Values are as important as either of those to ensure the whole business is on the same page. Getting on with these in an inclusive fashion is critical and they are best not being an agenda item for an hour at an awayday; creative design by committee is never a good idea. Mission, Vision and Values don't need to be perfect, but they will provide a consistent platform on which to refer and build.

One point to note is the miracles that can be achieved at an awayday by an expert facilitator can be achieved on a more routine and consistent basis by using an independent professional coach/mentor. When you can't see the answer yourself and it appears so easily as a result of interaction with others: that's what magic is.

Leadership team and board meetings are the key tool to communicate how you wish to operate and the culture you wish your reports to work within. I am familiar with attending leadership meetings where the agenda was followed by the CEO focusing on each department in turn, methodically machine-gunning around the room, one at a time. It was a consistent review of why something didn't happen and what the hell are you going to do about it, with a warning that it had better work by the next time. There was no cross-departmental debate with other directors – they were too busy wondering about how they were going to get away with their own section review. If you don't question the others, perhaps they won't lob unhelpful grenades in when it's your turn...

These meetings have little room for any positivity, and rarely look into the future or have any strategic input or direction. The one deviation may be getting a manager from the business who is running a key project to come and update the board on how it is going. This is generally scheduled for thirty minutes towards the end of the agenda. The poor manager who has been summoned is keen as mustard, sees it as a real opportunity to impress the CEO and board and has poured hours of unpaid overtime into the presentation to give his or her best. Inevitably, the agenda runs late and when, finally, the manager is invited in after hanging around for a long time, their boss says to them (sotto voce), 'Can you get through this in ten minutes – just cover the essentials...' All the hard work preparing is lost as they skip past painstakingly prepared slides and the chance to emphasise how important what they are doing is – to them and their team, as well as the wider company. All because there had been some forensic points scoring earlier about an operational detail that did not deserve a mention in a meeting of this magnitude.

Note: always put non-board member presenters, particularly those junior to the board, at the top of the agenda. Give them their time and compress or eliminate the nonsense at the back end of the meeting.

Assistants – the pièce de résistance

The other person to bear in mind as also critical, particularly when it is so lonely at the top, is your assistant, be they executive, personal assistant or secretary. Eugene Buckley had this to say to me: 'It's such a pivotal, trust-based relationship. They are often your filter to the organisation. I observed different dynamics and different PA stereotypes… It was always a good clue to the CEO's personality as to the character type of the PA.'

Much like any other appointment, this is an opportunity to bring skills that you lack or are disinterested in. Your executive assistant can also be a valued ear and a supportive confidante. They can boost your productivity massively and can learn to read your mind and second-guess almost everything. If the schedule you devised yourself won't actually work, they will have put it right before you've even asked. You left for that meeting without the key papers that you need for it, but they're already in your briefcase. Assistants can also be very useful at taking the temperature as to how things are going down with others in the office – what the mood is. Perhaps telling you the truths that others dare not.

I know other CEOs who have created a new position that is integral with their own and, therefore, increases the perception of their availability. For example, Martyn Gibbs hired a new business director who was process-driven and provided feedback that was aligned with his view as the CEO. This not only acted as a filter for the CEO to be able to give time to what was important, but also helped build trust with the organisation. People were able to ask 'daft questions' or suggest radical policies and solutions to someone other than the CEO. Also, comprehension of what was a significant, big-ticket item and what was more business as usual became more acute.

Keynote takeaway

Having the best relationship with your direct reports means delegation, and this should be meted out according to experience, ability and attitude – trust, in effect. And delegation across the whole business means, in a way, that you no longer run anything. You set the strategy and culture, you fire up and enthuse your people, you champion your company externally and you develop new business and partnerships that will build more success in both the short- and long-term. How liberating is that?

SEVEN

The Symphony Conductor

*Orchestrating success by managing
the wider company ensemble*

'We all live with the objective of being happy;
our lives are all different and yet the same.'
— Anne Frank

There is a story about Freddie Laker, the man who
built the eponymous low-cost, no-frills airline
offering cheap London–New York flights back in the
seventies and eighties. One day, walking through his
airline's premises, Laker noticed one of his employees had one shoe with the sole flapping from the bottom. Instead of ignoring the issue, he stopped and
asked the employee why he was wearing a broken
shoe. The employee explained that he couldn't afford
to buy a new pair of shoes (on what Laker was paying him) and that he'd tried to tape them up, but it
wasn't working very well. Without hesitation, Laker

reached into his pocket and fished out a big wad of banknotes. He extracted the notes from the large elastic band binding them together and then handed it to the employee, saying, 'Here, try this. It might help hold your shoe together until you can get a new pair.'

(There is an interesting and current postscript to this story. I thought I'd check Chat GPT as one way to verify the Freddie Laker anecdote, which sounds almost too good not to be apocryphal. The result was fantastic, in that it exposed AI as not yet being able to manage nuance and human emotions fully. Chat GPT gave me this: 'The story of Freddie Laker giving an elastic band to one of his employees has become something of a legend in the business world and it's often cited as an example of his compassion and generosity. Laker was known for being a hands-on boss who cared about his employees and was always willing to help them out when they needed it.')

SOS – band together to save our soles

The criticality of culture

The Freddie Laker story leads us to the point that generally, when one is discussing the wider company and particularly the relationship the CEO has with the employees, the word that everyone reaches for is 'culture'. This doesn't just happen, and it's harder to build than a major IT project or head office move as it not only needs everyone to engage, but it needs to be lived and breathed every day, all day. There's an excellent quote from Vistage's Chief Research Officer Joe Galvin who defines culture as '...your company's magnetic core – repelling employees who don't align with its tenets and attracting like-minded people who want to be part of it.'[36]

In the past, there were two directions that CEOs went in. Some chose to see their staff as a liability, though not many would own up to taking that view. It's probably not the first sentence read in most business books, but this line is consistently attributed to one publishing industry veteran who most people in the industry know: 'Never underestimate the ability of your staff to trash your business.'

A university pal I played rugby with as well as being a fine cricketer, Jake Pugh, has operated at the highest level as a consultant in the capital markets for over thirty years and been an MEP. He gave me the following insight:

'Through my consulting from 1997 to 2019, I worked at and in over fifty businesses. Because of the nature of the work I did, complex strategic change projects, I became a very keen observer of organisations and, in particular, the culture. Culture is the most important factor in any organisation. I think the oft-used expression is 'culture eats strategy for breakfast', and I completely agree.[37] There are only two organisations where I found the culture consistently positive. And, unsurprisingly, both businesses were hugely successful. Both had long term CEOs – over twenty years. Both were also founders/CEOs. In both of these financial services organisations, the CEO stayed influential in the business throughout. Longevity, clarity of thought, consistency and leadership were all essential.

'The other important element to me is teamwork. My brief sojourn into politics helped me to understand why our political class is often so inept and incompetent, and this is not a political point, they're all as bad as each other. In all my time in politics, which has continued to some extent since 2020, I've never met a single politician, or inhabitant of SW1, who has ever played any team sport! No wonder we're where we are...'

According to this, being a long-standing CEO, over twenty years in situ, is more likely to breed a positive culture than being a first-time CEO. How then do the newcomers try and achieve this in short order? First, decide what you wish the culture to be, and second, walk the walk. Deloitte's Dan Oakey again:

> 'Culture is basically information on how to behave that we glean from our environment and peers. What does it take to succeed in your tribe? Who do you need to impress? Which of the thousands of rules and strictures do you really need to obey? Your staff are looking to you for clues on how to behave – everything you do (or don't do) sends them a message on how to get on. Any functional head transgressing their own rules will go viral.'

The end of Prime Minister Boris Johnson after Partygate would seem to verify this.[38]

Where to start

New CEOs also need to get out there and talk to people. More importantly, they need to listen to them. But, how to prioritise who you should be listening to? First off, the previous CEO if they are available, followed by the chair and members of the board and your fellow directors on the Senior Leadership Team. We've covered these in the last couple of chapters. Now it's time for the staff: individuals, groups and teams across the whole company, whether it's within the same building or those working remotely at the nether end of your business' outposts. Go out and meet, talk and listen to them. Show them that you are happy to listen and that they and their views are valued. Create a culture of honesty and one where you welcome input, challenge, ideas and even criticism – this applies at all levels. The culture that welcomes the best ideas rather than the one that agrees with the CEO is a winning culture.

The best ideas tend to come from those working within the business – the people who are closest to the detail and can see efficiencies in processes or systems that would be transformative to how they do their jobs and how their output could be dramatically improved. The right culture will not only encourage them to put their ideas forward, it will have them caring about doing better for the company and its interests, and will actually incentivise them by rewarding and recognising them for doing so.

As an example, fear of failure is a huge inhibitor. Sports fans can contrast the whole Eddie Jones era in charge of the England Men's Rugby Team post the 2019 Rugby World Cup versus the concept of 'Bazball' as adopted by the English Men's Cricket Test Team under Head Coach Brendon McCullum. England Women's Football Head Coach Sarina Wiegman transformed the national team through liberating and trusting her players and the 'Lionesses' are followed by millions more fans as a result. It is incredible what can be achieved when this fear is removed and the shackles taken off.

During my many years as a director, at one point I took over a new department dealing with exports that I was unfamiliar with. My inexperience in the specialism was massively outweighed by my decision to meet all ten or so members of this team individually for an hour's chat to find out about and listen to them. This was mentioned by them and their manager several times, particularly pointing out that no one responsible for the team at my level had ever done that before. They felt genuinely valued as a result. This was a high-performing team and remained so. Being treated as respected and appreciated colleagues will have contributed in some way and is something anyone can adopt as an approach from day one, no matter the number of years under your belt. And this works at every level.

When it comes to attracting and retaining the best talent and leaders to come and work at your company, the culture could well be the defining factor.

There's possibly also a lesson here about not always taking yourself too seriously. Yes, you need to look and act the part, but giving others a glimpse of a level of humanity and a sense of humour are fine. Glen Ward is an ex-colleague in the UK who has been a serial CEO on the west coast in California for the last twenty-five years. He told me a lovely story about his first days as a CEO:

'As an ex-pat Brit, who had been appointed recently as CEO of the Virgin Entertainment Group in North America, I was relishing the prospect of expanding our unique Megastore offering and finding suitable new locations in which to plant our flag and show how music retail should be done. Within a few weeks of starting, I received a call at my office in Los Angeles from our commercial real estate advisor asking me to meet him in St Louis to tread the streets and visit a few promising properties currently on the market. I relished the prospect of seeing other parts of the country and quickly arranged to fly out the following week.

'I was scheduled to be greeted "downtown" by my advisor and a group of property folks, but arrived early for our meeting, so went and sat in a local restaurant near to our rendezvous point to grab a coffee and continue reading up about the local market. One thing that intrigued me though, was the pronunciation of the city's name. Was it Saint Louis (French accented version); Saint Louis (hard 's' US version); or Saint Louis (soft 's' US version)? Not wanting to offend the locals, I thought I'd ask the waitress to enlighten me. As she walked by, I said, "Excuse me, but how do

I pronounce this place we are in?" She gave me a somewhat bemused look and then, very deliberately and rather pityingly, replied, 'MC...Don...alds!" So, my first two lessons as a CEO: always remain humble, and do your homework before asking a question.'

Company culture is individual but can change

Don't underestimate the power and weight of the culture in a company and how different this may be from others you have worked in.

I worked at HMV for twelve years and the culture was 'work hard, play hard', with the focus on operational efficiency driven by a JFDI approach in a blokey, and occasionally sexist, atmosphere. If something needed doing urgently then the whip was cracked and it was delivered pronto. It was this operational slickness that gave HMV dominance over the sexier Virgin brand. It may also have contributed to a lack of humility, curiosity and strategic vision when it came to online, digital and streamed content which so decimated traditional retailers across many sectors. Though HMV collapsed into administration in 2013, I'm glad to say it is still trading in the UK today.

When I moved to Waterstones, I learned the hard way just how different the cultures were. Of the staff, over

90% had university degrees, and far more women worked in head office and ran the stores than in HMV. The operational duties working in a store were often not the highest of their personal priorities. If something needed doing, any directive from head office needed to fully explain *why*. The rationale was important and the engagement and buy-in of the store staff was hard won and essential. JFDI had the opposite effect.

The two chains of stores were both trading entertainment products that the staff loved and were the reason most people had joined, yet they could not have been more different. Several senior HMV people had transferred to Waterstones and the ones who struggled and failed tended to automatically implement policies and procedures that had worked in HMV. The ones who succeeded tended to listen to the experienced Waterstones staff more or learned more quickly from their own mistakes. I believe my breakthrough with the store staff was at an annual conference when I took responsibility and personally apologised for a (particularly daft) promotional campaign that the previous MD had instigated. I said that I wished I could replay my first year at the company and listen and learn more from the experienced Waterstones staff. My distaste at copping it for someone else's foolish decision was more than compensated for by issuing what was apparently the first apology the stores had received from head office in years and the respect that this generated.

The importance of communication

The one constant in all this is communication. At the basic level, this does not have to be complicated. The armed forces consider simple and straightforward communication as critical and have an ingenuous philosophy when it comes to comms. In fact, this is based on the three Aristotle principles outlined 2,500 years ago:

1. Tell them what you are going to say.

2. Tell them.

3. Tell them what you told them.

Getting the message across is key, and anyone listening should be able to relay that message when asked what the communication was about.

This is speech-making level one and there are much more gripping ways to address your audience with framing stories, a real narrative and an obvious passion for the subject. Not forgetting letting the audience know *why* they are there. If you are not confident in this area, go on a course or get help. Salma Ibrahim is CEO of both Literary Natives and Miro Digital. She explains:

> 'Being able to communicate effectively as a leader, not just through the good times but the bad times too, is something that is seldom

taught anywhere in my experience. It seems counterintuitive; you're selected to lead a team or project because you're deemed as someone who has the ability to make it work, so showing that you're struggling seems like a step backwards. I struggled to communicate the challenges and failures with my team, and thus my impostor syndrome grew quietly. I believed my team was only interested in progressing a project and reaching key milestones and that I would make myself look like a weak leader by letting them know what I was finding difficult.

'It took me some time to learn that there was so much wisdom and power in being transparent, sharing my struggles with capacity and processes and highlighting where I wanted to seek more expertise. I learned to humanise myself in this process. Leaders don't know it all. We aren't expected to. We become better leaders by owning up to that and sharing our journey.'

As well as being sincere, consistent and authentic, for those who enjoy crafting public speaking, it's worth attending a course on some fundamental principles in constructing a good speech. The best structural building blocks can make the rhetoric sing off the page and sweep the audience along in a more cohesive and convincing manner. Tips such as telling a story, the

'Rule of Three', how to use repetition, as well as metaphors, similes, and even phrasing such as alliteration (ironically), anadiplosis, antimetabole, antithesis, asyndeton (just to mention the 'A's!) are easy to absorb and utilise. Careful and measured use of these techniques can really give your speech the emphasis and gravitas that help messages to land. Without going into additional steps that are critical to master public speaking, the most important is to make sure you rehearse your speech out loud. If doing it in front of colleagues or others, concentrate on what it is that you're saying – the content – rather than the emphasis or style of delivery. But don't leave out on rehearsing the delivery too – even if just to yourself. It's no fun to hear yourself say 'hyperbowl' out loud during a speech when you were looking for 'hyperbole'!

It's not just how you say it, but when, and with what frequency. I've illustrated earlier that a lack of communication creates a vacuum that breeds paranoia and conspiracy theories, where the assumption can be to fear the worst. I explained earlier that while I was CEO of Borders, our US parent company announced that they were 'exploring strategic alternatives', meaning us overseas territories were, to all intents and purposes, for sale. My priorities as the leader changed immediately to two basic things in addition to the sale process of the company. I had to keep every member of staff engaged and on board, as it's easy to become a poacher's target under those circumstances and lose your best people. I also had to focus even harder on the company's current performance to ensure that our sales, profit, balance sheet and cash were in good order to try and maximise the value of any sale for our US parent company.

The key to this was through communication. Rumours and gossip were rife and there was much conjecture about who might buy us or whether we might perhaps be allowed to go under. I decided to issue a personal staff bulletin every Friday to be put up in every store, office and distribution facility that we had.

Some of the conjecture still swilled around and was sometimes originated on the basis of fact, but the conclusions that resulted were pure fantasy. I am sure that every single one of our competitors applied to enter the data room and take a good look at our numbers, but that didn't mean that they were serious contenders or even interested in buying us. The crucial point of my weekly communication to the company was to say *something* and keep the dialogue open, even if it was primarily one way. Some weeks there would be little to say and others there might have been some major activity, but it was inappropriate to share it at that point. The actual content of the communication was less important than the fact that it was happening. There was no vacuum, and its absence meant that the conditions were not as conducive for a negative culture to build and thrive than there might have been otherwise.

Keynote takeaway

It's all about culture and communication. I made the point earlier that this was not a book where billionaires would cast pearls before the rest of us, but I will allow one quote from Richard Branson because its simplicity means anyone can adopt it: 'There's no magic formula for great company culture. The key is just to treat your staff how you would like to be treated.'[39]

PART THREE
EXTERNAL RELATIONSHIPS

EIGHT
Client Chemistry
Nurturing irresistible relationships
as a savvy CEO

'If I am selling to you, I speak your language.
If I am buying, dann müssen sie Deutsch sprechen.'
— Willy Brandt, former Chancellor of
West Germany

When I joined Waterstones, my first job was to introduce myself to all the publishers. At the same time, I had to ask them to take back fifteen million pounds worth of 'dead' stock that we were sitting on. We had bought it all on 100% sale or return but frittered away our contracted right to return it through our poor processes, inaccurate administration and inefficiency. Nonetheless, it represented cash and we needed to liquidate it. 'Hi, I'm David, very nice to meet you. I need you to do something for me please...'

Some publishers went for this, most wanted a new order to the same value in return for taking their stock back, and a few asked for an order of double the value of the returns, but generally a deal was done. There was only one publisher who refused outright. Their MD listened to my pitch and told me that, 'It was not in the interest of our shareholders to accept the Waterstones' dead stock back.' There's a time and a place to use a dominant market share which Waterstones had then, and particularly when what's offered is a flat refusal rather than a conversation, and everyone else is playing ball. I told him that Waterstones would not buy another book from them and, if necessary, would return all their current stock in our stores that we were entitled to. The MD listened to this and then said that in light of this, 'It is now in the interest of our shareholders to accept Waterstones' dead stock back.'

This chapter looks at the relationships with key companies and contacts either side of you in the supply chain – suppliers and clients. It's easily arguable that these are also 'partners', but we'll look at a different definition of these in the next chapter.

Your position in the food chain

Working with clients and suppliers can be very different, depending on which end of the food chain you are on. As someone who worked with and ran buying teams through a good chunk of their retail career before general management, I would concur it is easier to be a buyer than a seller and that I was more comfortable on that side of the fence. Caveat emptor, yes, but it was generally the far easier side of the table to be on. If someone wanted to sell you something, you could always say no and an improved offer was likely to follow. If you were already their customer, then they had something to lose if you withdrew.

I remember attending a negotiation skills course along with a few people from other industries. Among other things, this included being filmed while attempting a sales pitch. Once I had completed this element, I was asked if I worked on the 'buying' side of the fence rather than the 'sales' side. It turned out I was the only such person on the course and was rather easily identified as such through my body language on the video. On watching the video back, I saw myself sat back in my chair while pitching and I had my arms crossed in front of me throughout. The power of saying no was already deeply ingrained, even if unsuitable for this particular task in hand.

The difference between the approach of one supplier and another was mostly obvious and those who treated the relationship as a partnership and were happy to plan the relationship together stood out. At HMV, I think of our relationship with EMI Classics as a very simple example. We had only a dozen or more major city centre stores who could legitimately offer a credible range of classical music, but outside of that, the market was patchy at best. In addition, each store's knowledge of classical music and the range to stock in their town was equally erratic. Bearing in mind that music was bought with a cap of around 5% on returns, this was a risky venture and tied up cash if you got it wrong.

As a result, we worked with EMI to repackage many of their fabulous recordings into an 'HMV Classics' range that allowed us to stock a balanced, though limited, range within a set number of linear feet within most of our stores. Everyone would have Beethoven's 5th and 9th Symphonies, Dvořák's 'New World' and Mozart's 'Requiem', but only one version of each and on our own label with the guaranteed terms and margin around that. If a classical album hit the chart in its own right, such as Nigel Kennedy's version of Vivaldi's *Four Seasons*, then that's where it was merchandised. We sold over a million CDs of our HMV Classics range over the next five years or so and it was a big success for both HMV and EMI.

In the case of both clients and suppliers, it's important to step into their shoes. What is important to them and what is it they are hoping to get out of this discussion/negotiation/deal? At Waterstones, we wished to

*Classic memories – over 1 million units
sold in this collection with EMI*

grow our margin in a way that reflected the business that we did with publishers, the support that we gave across their lists and the market share that we held at that time. If I could present data that showed us being responsible for the entire growth within a sector, which we often could, that helped. As above, it always made a big difference to me if these conversations were met with a flat refusal – the supplier's sole aim was to not give any more points of percentage margin away. Much more productive for both parties were the conversations that explored what they would get in return, whether there were conditions or targets linked to the attainment of improved terms and whether the achievement of targets triggered one-off payments or file term increases for the future. All these were valid variables and meant a discussion could begin. Were there any areas of their business that needed greater support or were there new authors, bands, franchises or products that they had invested in that they wished to plan into our schedule?

Premature escalation

I never went to war with a supplier who entered into a discussion, and I always initiated the discussion by trying to find out what was important to them.

The market share that you possess and can wield is, of course, a major factor. When I moved from Waterstones to become CEO of Borders, this difference was dramatic and required a different way of using leverage than I had performed before. I was very glad at that point that I had not abused the clout that I had while at Waterstones and was seen as a hard but fair negotiator who delivered on my side of the bargain. If I had thrown my weight around willy-nilly earlier, I would have got short shrift at Borders if I had come to the table this time with more of a begging bowl than a Christmas stocking.

The biggest surprise of all was the consideration from the supplier side. Up until the mid-noughties, publishers would freely admit that they saw their customers as the book chains and indie bookshops, not the readers and fans of their authors. No real consideration was given to the end consumers. Given everything that any company produces or offers ultimately depends on its attractiveness to the end consumer, this is unusual. In an industry that offers booksellers 100% sale or return, you might think it doubly so. In this book, I'm specifically looking at the focused relationships with your company's everyday contacts rather than the relationship with the consumer. That's a book in itself, and so we'll park it here.

What does it take to be the best client or supplier to the other party's supplier/client? How can you contribute as a first-time CEO to these relationships which are likely managed by one of your direct reports on a day-to-day basis?

The basic principle is to make clear what it is that your company is trying to achieve (mission, vision, etc) and for both parties to understand what their purpose is. In an ideal world, these would have parallels or connections that mean your relationship can progress you both along towards your desired directions. Such perception and clarity are obviously key when assessing your client's needs, but this is not always considered in a similar way with your suppliers. This understanding is critical when it comes to planning your work together on a periodic or annual basis, or longer. There are multiple occasions when supporting one product or supplier over another may be a fifty-fifty call for your company; there's not much in it and the difference may mean little to you, at least relatively. This is where building in the desired support into an overall plan can make such a difference to your supplier – it's small beer for you but a major deal for them. Offering this in advance can also enable confident planning and investment which will benefit both parties.

Understanding what your supplier's priorities and key moments are can be massive for them and virtually business as usual for you. It's reverse account management, if you like, and all the more powerful for it.

Standing up for what is rightfully yours

The customer is always right – unless they're not. There are dream clients who may do business with you in the way described above. There may also be others who jerk your chain in an unacceptable way. Paying promptly for goods or services received can be one such area. The easiest way for companies to alleviate any pinch points in their annual cashflow is to just let the payment slip a cycle from, say, thirty days to sixty days. Unsurprisingly, this tends to be activated on accounts where the balance of power is firmly in the client's favour and the recipient is too small to be able to wield any great retribution that might damage the late payer. That means the suppliers who probably can least afford to be without the cash in their bank for the late period – any freelancers will be familiar with this.

I was told a story by Alice Edgcumbe-Rendle, CEO of Edgcumbe Tea and Coffee Ltd, a successful SME based in Sussex who have been giving excellent service to their community and clients for over forty years. In a former life, she was responsible for sales into the trade of a well-known beer that was aimed at curry lovers, particularly in restaurants at its outset. One account proved problematic, with the business changing hands and the new owner relinquishing their responsibility for the debts they had inherited (this was not a bankruptcy). With the refusal of this restaurant to settle what it owed, Alice arranged for a day trip to the restaurant for her team and accountant to have a slap-up meal with the aim being that they try and arrive at a bill that approximated to what was owed by the restaurant.

They arrived by minibus and after a feast of specials and all the sides, when presented with the bill, Alice asked her accountant to present copies of all the outstanding invoices and declared that she estimated that given the outstanding debt and the restaurant bill that they had just run up, she owed them £10 and put a tenner on the table. Bedlam ensued and the police were called, but the pragmatic line was taken at the time that this seemed a reasonable balance and the restaurant owner was persuaded not to press charges. It's an old-school story, set in times that were different than today, but I'm sure that the invoices were paid more promptly following this rather drastic action! Alice is convinced word spread around the restaurant community and payments were more prompt across the board as a result.

It's best to work in tandem with one's clients and suppliers, but the more this is treated as a partnership of equals, the better it will work. Having one side take the piss makes it fair play for the other to call them on it. This is more likely to gain respect than to be seen as desperately scrabbling for money owed.

The supplier relationship can vary. Two examples in my time that have similarities but differ wildly in effect and influence were Warner Bros and Amazon. When DVD was launched in the UK, Warner Bros Home Entertainment (as it was known) was determined to be the main DVD player when the format was launched and had sent over one of their brightest rising stars, Ron Sanders, to head the company and the launch strategy. The home video landscape hadn't left the legacy of a smooth platform for DVD to launch from, and all the players were haggling for position. VHS had knocked out its (possibly better) Betamax competitor, and with DVD the film companies were trying individually to find the right price point. They couldn't even agree on the best case to house the format, with the US launching with an extended case to try and utilise the existing browsers in retail stores; in the UK, Warners put their product in a cardboard 'snapper' case, while Polygram (now Universal) and Columbia used an extended jewel case, similar to how music CDs are housed. All were awful and flimsy and did no justice to the new format.

I mentioned earlier that at HMV we were 100% behind the new format and saw DVD as transformational – we were determined to back it from day one and become market leader overnight. I also mentioned that we had to fend off an attempt by the film companies to use the new format to re-align the terms across both chart and back catalogue to favour their side of the table. Through careful management, pushing back, refusing to be railroaded and working closely with Warner Bros, we managed to not only come to market with a fantastic offering, but we also helped to create a highly profitable growth sector for the market.

Be cute about your strengths not Canute against the tide

Amazon is another topic for a book in itself, but here I just want to cover its position within the publishing industry back in the late noughties and the perception of the company as a 'frenemy'. Amazon had built its initial offer and format on books, providing publishers with a revolutionary way to distribute their deep backlist and long tail directly to customers. It then created the market leading eBook reader, the Kindle, to enable people to take their collection of digital books with them wherever they went – a godsend for those of us who needed additional luggage on planes just to accommodate our to-be-read list on holiday. Alongside its cloud and marketplace businesses, it then developed itself as a publisher, offering its Kindle Direct Publishing services to authors as well as opening imprints designed to take on the traditional publishers. As an aside, it was planning to open physical bookstores too, having seduced many of the bookshop chains in the UK to hand over their customers during the previous few years by providing them with a white label online store. Disruption? You bet.

When I joined HarperCollins Publishing in late 2008, one thing was clear: Amazon were the one customer with the potential to grow massively in a short space of time. With the right focus and a partnership approach, we could grow our business incrementally and very quickly in ways that would also increase their market share significantly. We would be feeding the beast that might turn round and eat us, along with our fellow publishers, if they were allowed to grow their business, their author community, their consumer base, and their ambition. We discussed this at a top level on many an occasion, as did the rest of the industry. And, like all of us, the seductive attraction of the top line and the invoice generation of orders always won the day. To paraphrase Mike Tyson's earlier quote: 'Everyone has a plan until a big order comes in.' Over the previous ten years there had been a similar story of seduction as the supermarkets were able to reach new customers and provide incremental sales, though the discounts they demanded were high and the price points they sold books at were low, potentially devaluing the product.

Making sure that we shared the growth benefits with Amazon was key and I was delighted to agree a three-year deal that I believe was unique at the time to HarperCollins. This would see Amazon rewarded with one-off payments for certain growth targets and potentially having their file terms (the standard discount applied to all their base business with us – the holy grail for retailers) increased if the highest targets were achieved. I was pleased to see over time that we had set these pretty much spot on with the actual growth falling between the two, giving us significant, profitable growth without moving the margin bar detrimentally on an ongoing basis. Of course, this didn't last forever and as I was leaving HarperCollins a couple of years later, I know Amazon were trying to rip up the remainder of the three-year deal as 'it wasn't working for them'. Their increased market share and growing dominance made this something that had to be considered despite the ink on the deal.

Deloitte did a study in 2023 that showed 69% of procurement executives believed that supplier relationships have a significant impact on their company's competitive advantage.[40] No sh*t, Sherlock – what were the other 31% thinking?! And procurement execs consider themselves the 'orchestrators of value'? Companies with strong supplier relationships experience 2.5 times greater supplier performance compared to those with weak relationships,[41] so it's worth investing the time.

Clients and suppliers may provide the content for your livelihood or your route to market and consumers. They will affect turnover and margin and determine both your top and your bottom lines. With this influence on your business, doesn't it seem sensible that the CEO should do anything necessary to improve these relationships rather than just leave it to the buying or sales director? Getting involved – as appropriate and agreed with the functional head who owns the relationship – is important and worth the time. Establishing a relationship with their CEO is also important as it builds the trust and empathy between the ultimate decision makers. When I was made Product Director at HMV, my first negotiation was with Sony Music, home of Michael Jackson, Whitney Houston and Bruce Springsteen. Their long-standing Sales Director, who had previously dealt directly with our MD, sat back and laconically and condescendingly asked 'So, what has your MD told you to ask for?' to which I responded, 'Probably a little but more than your MD has told that you can give me.' We both knew that we moved the pieces, but the final decision rested with the person at the top.

Keynote takeaway

We are dependent on the creators and originators, in-house or external, and those who pay for our products or services. The most important of these relationships must be in the orbit of the CEO rather than totally outsourced to a member of their team.

NINE

Alliance Amplification

Embracing partnerships as your company's supercharged extensions

'A friendship founded on business is better than a business founded on friendship.'
— John D Rockefeller

It's a given that we have partnerships with our clients and suppliers. In this chapter, however, I am referring to partners – meaning those who provide services or products that help us extend our business rather than those who sell us things that we, in turn, sell, or those who buy our products from us. These are not our neighbours in the supply chain but people who enable us to do our job better and reach more customers. These may range from a large, all service advertising agency to a freelance publicist, or from one of the top four recruitment agencies to a one-person headhunter specialist.

The difference between these partners and clients and suppliers is that their agenda should align perfectly with yours – your success will reflect well on them – and, ideally, their remuneration is aligned to it too. Clients and suppliers are different – they want you to sell/buy loads of their products, but they have others who will do the same; the better the margin for you, the tighter it may be for them.

With alignment, genuine partners should be treated as one of the team in a similar way to your company's own employees.

The brief that you give them is critical for them to be able to produce the right answer and their knowledge of your culture and way of working is essential if they are going to deliver for you in the way you wish.

As the overall project manager, I remember well the first project meeting when HMV took on Capgemini to support our massive systems rollout across store Epos, inventory and finance systems. The consultant kicked off the inaugural meeting and immediately tried to impose a fine on all late arrivals to establish the importance of prompt attendance to these weekly meetings from the outset. This was something that just did not work in that culture – having the key people attend at all at the outset was a big win! This needed reversing and commitment being secured in a way that sought buy-in rather than slapping naughty boys on the wrist. Capgemini's approach from the starting gun may have worked wonderfully well with other customers but it had the opposite effect here.

Fast forward thirty years to today and I am lucky enough to chair the writing agency New Writing North, whose remit is to develop writers and readers of all ages across the north of England. NWN is based in Newcastle upon Tyne, where we have produced nationally significant work since 1996. We help excellent writing find local, regional, national and international audiences. This is a company that lives and breathes partnerships, as it is entirely dependent on them: from Arts Council England, who provide around 22% of our funding, to Northumbria University, who sponsor much of our Northern Writers Awards programme and Hachette Publishing, who we partner with to deliver an MA in Publishing degree. Additionally, there are dozens of engaged and highly talented freelance professionals who deliver programmes in schools and across the region.

I have seen a lot of partnerships in action with companies that I have worked for and across industries where I have sat at the top of their trade associations. I can safely say that New Writing North is the best at creating partnerships that I have come across. Essential at the beginning is the ambition to address an issue or chase a goal, sometimes in areas where, 'Been there, tried, that – didn't work,' is the typical result. By definition, these are generally problems that need tackling and, therefore, need persistence and different approaches before they are successfully challenged.

The key is to keep the focus of all parties on the result you are trying to achieve at all times.

The political shenanigans along the way are secondary and a distraction, and the possessiveness of ideas and ownership will divert attention. The only important thing is solving the problem you all set out to achieve. To attract the interest of multiple parties is a great achievement. To keep them all on track in a single-minded way is rare. To do so consistently across a wide range of local and national initiatives is unique. This is achieved not so much by training and business processes, but by words like passion, pragmatism, focus, communication, empathy, enthusiasm, ambition, drive and determination. I am full of admiration for Claire Malcolm, NWN's CEO, and Anna Disley, Deputy CEO, along with their team. They are an example to much bigger organisations on how to achieve great things by collaboration.

Knowing what you bring to the party

As the junior partner in a relationship, it's important to understand the needs of the dominant partner and how you can support them in achieving their goals. Several years ago, I worked as a NED with a startup company who produced an app which delivered a digital copy of books onto phones or tablets and then deleted them once they had been read. The idea was that the books would be slightly cheaper at a normal app price as the reader was borrowing rather than buying and owning them. However, they could then pass one copy of the book for free onto a named friend within their Facebook group, in a similar way to how you might pass on a paperback that you had enjoyed. The ability to share and the number of free copies allowed in that way could be controlled by the publisher, so these features ticked the 'IP protection' and 'control' boxes that were so important to them.

Though this was designed as a direct-to-consumer sales app, it was flawed by the fact that people are not generally in purchasing mode when on Facebook and the company had a limited amount of cash that meant only a couple of further iterations of the app were possible before they would go bust. Getting quality book content early on for the app from publishers was critical. During that time, I introduced them to, among others, the deputy CEO of Random House. They immediately saw the potential for superfans of certain best-selling authors to become the advocates who would target hand-picked new readers who would become, in turn, the next fans to work through the authors' backlist and become advocates themselves. This was particularly attractive for those authors who it was felt may be reaching saturation point in the UK despite only a small fraction of the adult population having read them. They saw the app as a marketing platform rather than a direct-to-customer sales app, and they were right.

On this basis, Random House then floated the idea that we utilise the functionality that we had developed to build apps for both James Patterson and Dan Brown. Working with the world's biggest trade publisher on a project with the world's two best-selling authors – what's not to like, you might think? In response, the app company's founder and CEO rejected this proposal and insisted that the original strategy of direct-to-customer sales via social media was the right one and we should continue to develop the app. Really? I discontinued my association immediately and the company fizzled out when the cash ran dry a couple of months later.

There can be a perfect point to pivot, but you need to be live enough to see it and recognise it as such.

It's generally not as obvious as global names asking you to work with them, but it should not be a question of pride or criticism – quite the opposite, it can be the butterfly emerging from the cocoon.

The importance of no

Having said that, one art that takes time to develop and is often only learned from experience is how to say *no*. This is particularly difficult if you are starting your own business, perhaps as a consultant or freelancer, and need the turnover. Any turnover. When you are starting out on your own there can be a few contacts that just want to pick your brains or mine your knowledge and experience, especially if you are fresh from working with a competitor of theirs. This may include startups that want to utilise your address book and who are unable to pay you for your time and experience but offer a share in their future success. There's no harm in picking examples who have an interesting proposition, but you do need to select your horses carefully. There are only so many times that you can play this card and take up the time of important and influential people you have spent years cultivating and who value your judgement.

I learned the hard way when introducing a guy who lived in the south of France and had developed a way of producing bespoke design products that could be enhanced with branding from, in this case, favourite literary characters. It was an interesting proposition as these quality products were made to order in short time and at reasonable cost. I arranged a meeting with a children's publisher who had some interesting licences and even took the precaution of looking at his presentation deck and making some appropriate adjustments. However, when we got to the meeting, the first thing he did, to my amazement, was to produce a manuscript of a children's book that he had written and proceed to pitch it to the publisher. I was obviously mortified, and it took much apologising and grovelling on my part to try and put that right.

Timing can play a huge part and provide luck in any launch or decision to pivot but it's the recognition of the right moment that is the skill. HMV decided to enter the mail order industry back in the nineties when Britannia Music was the dominant player in the music direct-mail market. Once we announced that we were starting this new venture, Britannia thought that their days were numbered. HMV had the clout with the record companies and the trusted brand with consumers to be able to walk in and push the established players out. We took on a premises to handle the distribution and direct-to-customer fulfilment and then worked on the launch and marketing plan. This centred on the production of a relatively lavish hardback book which was designed to sit on a coffee table and be dipped into by discerning customers who would flick through and select a CD to purchase when they had one of those, 'Ooh, I feel like buying a CD; let's look in the HMV Direct book,' moments (me neither).

Once this book had been launched, Britannia and the other mail order companies who had assumed they were finished, breathed a huge sigh of relief. HMV could have wiped them off the face of the map, but had misread how to approach the mail order market, despite some high-profile, specialist advice. HMV were trying to attract a more discerning demographic, but other mail order players knew that price was key, subscriptions were necessary and you needed to bombard your customers with offers on a frequent basis through well-thumbed media. With a disparity of pricing with the stores that was taken as unwelcome rivalry by HMV retail staff, and a drive for immediate payback rather than a longer-term investment criterion, HMV and its backers didn't have the patience to let this new venture find its offer and its market. As it was, the business was shut down after a couple of years.

The postscript to this story is that this was all before the emergence of Amazon beyond it just selling books. HMV had the facilities in place to distribute individual CDs direct to customers in 1996 and were ahead of Amazon by two months in fulfilling internet orders for online customers for music. This pivot to a market that proved to be enormous was not given the time to prove itself, however. How things might have been different in the UK if HMV had got the mail order partnership flying from the off and had, as a result, persevered, built and transformed their business over time as the new online market emerged. It has been suggested to me that, given the extraordinary dot-com bubble that inflated over the next couple of years, HMV Direct may have been worth as much as its bricks and mortar sister businesses within that short period of time.

Sliding Doors: HMV Direct Catalogue volume 1, 1996

Continually assessing the value of partnerships

Knowing when a partnership has run its course is also important. It's also probably a measure of the worth of the partner in question too. It's a cliché, but an average partner can get comfortable after a couple of years and even start to load the invoicing on occasion. Most partners will work hard initially to get the account and may discount the opening offer to secure the business. This can add up when looking at the total turnover that will be amassed over the life of the partnership, assuming perhaps that this lasts at least three or more years. The sensible company that is paying for the partnership will have some control over their governance in the procurement arena that reviews relationships on a regular, ongoing basis, to keep everyone on their toes. Such practices may be best kept at arm's length from those who own the relationship, as they may also get comfortable with the relationship which has taken perhaps years to develop to the point where the partner understands the brand and culture of your organisation. Originating a brief and starting again with a beauty parade and induction of a new agency, for example, is hard work and time consuming, with no guaranteed beneficial results. Though, it might just be the practice itself that means your incumbent partners keep giving of their best.

It can also happen that partnerships and the expertise that you need are available and right under your nose. HarperCollins are best known for their Trade business division which hosts a stable of authors from JRR Tolkien and George RR Martin to Agatha Christie, Hilary Mantel and David Walliams. As with all publishers, the advent of digital transformation and eBooks was a huge question and focus of attention in the noughties. The CEO was constantly asking where we could learn from and how we should tackle this problem and opportunity. Rather less known were the other divisions within HarperCollins: one specialising in mapping, one in dictionaries and one in education. All of which had been through a sizeable digital transformation over the previous decade, and in the case of mapping and dictionaries, now had the vast majority of their business trading in digital products. Whether this was too close to see properly or deemed irrelevant for the Trade business, back then HarperCollins never seemed to interrogate internally to extract the lessons between different divisions of the same business.

This used to also be true for the relationship with its sister companies within the News Corporation empire. Everyone would proudly say that at HarperCollins we were working for and were part of the UK's third biggest publisher (behind Random House and Hachette at the time). When I joined, I would ask why we didn't say we worked for and were part of the world's biggest media empire? Publishing types tend to lean left politically, but the association with Rupert Murdoch to me was outweighed by the opportunity our association provided us. We had IP and our partner organisations included film companies, TV stations, cable networks, satellite TV and newspapers. Did we leverage the relationships with our next-door neighbours? We did not at that time. After the split into two divisions and the move of HarperCollins' head office into the same building as *The Times* and *The Sun*, this has developed considerably, as one would expect.[42]

Knowing the moment of truth is also a skill beyond most people, particularly when it is at a transformational stage of not just a company but an industry as a whole. The Time Warner merger with AOL in 2001 at $350 billion was the biggest ever US corporate merger.[43] It is used in business schools as a disaster example and is generally seen as a newcomer with an inflated stock price cashing in by buying an established player with tangible assets and content.

One that went the other way was the story of Blockbuster who rented VHS tapes to millions of people who wanted to watch movies in the comfort of their own homes.[44] In 1997, Blockbuster had a global business with 9,000 stores in the US alone and a turnover of $6 billion. A startup called Netflix had established an online DVD rental subscription service through the post but were losing money hand over fist. Their co-founders arranged a meeting with Blockbuster's executives and proposed that Blockbuster should buy Netflix for $50 million. With Blockbuster's retail estate and customer base coupled with Netflix managing the online arm, they felt that the combination would be worth more than the individual parts. Blockbuster did not take this smaller startup as a serious threat to their market dominance and the Netflix duo were laughed out the building. The rest is history. Blockbuster went bust in 2010 and Netflix is worth $187 billion today.

In the last chapter, I mentioned how important it was that the CEO had a stake in the key relationships and how critical the CEO-to-CEO relationships are. Often, the best connections are made via partnerships that have a direct influence on how your company, and, therefore, you perform. These allow you access to connections and audiences that you would otherwise not reach, they can provide scale and resource that you need to meet your goals and they may have expertise that you do not have inhouse.

Keynote takeaway

Building partnerships can be the most powerful way to amplify what you do, buying in specialist expertise that you don't have the time or money to develop inhouse. That doesn't mean that you should not invest the required amount of money into hiring the right partners for you or spend the required time to ensure that they are working in tandem and with the full knowledge of your brand, offer and customers. Properly aligned, these partners will become as important as your own team.

Industry Luminary

*Elevating your CEO standing in
the wider business cosmos*

'I've searched all the parks in all the cities
and found no statues of committees.'
— Gilbert K Chesterton

G etting everyone in your company onside is obviously the priority, followed by cementing the best relationships with your most important clients, suppliers and partners. The next dimension to address is the wider industry that you work in. As a first-time CEO, you may well be a key person of influence within your industry already, or you may be an 'outsider' who has no previous experience or profile in the sector. Either way, becoming a key player in your current industry will benefit both your company and you.

When I moved from HMV to Waterstones, I was moving from being relatively well known in the music and film world to being a newbie in the book one. Because of my role, I was offered a seat on the Booksellers Association (BA) Council which was the board that ran the industry's trade association for retailers and libraries across the UK and Ireland. This was an excellent way to meet other major players in the sector and my peers within other major retailers as well as influential independent bookshop owners who had been around for ages. Waterstones had been a member of the BA for years and much of the unpopularity that they may have had when opening stores and effectively closing independent bookshops in towns had evaporated by this point. Amazon had just left the BA and supermarkets were being encouraged to sit on the council at this point so there were more pressing concerns than attacking other bookselling specialists. Still, the expectation was that we would throw our weight around and look after our own interests at the expense of the wider trade.

At my first meeting, we discussed the release of the most anticipated new books and how the biggest players such as Waterstones and WH Smith put these titles out on sale as soon as they received them, often several days prior to the official publication date. This gave us an unfair advantage compared with the independent bookshops who probably didn't get their delivery of these big titles until the day before. One independent bookshop owner suggested that we could perhaps introduce an embargo until the publication date to give a level playing field to the industry and provide the marketeers with an opportunity to build anticipation and hype among the public about the release date in a similar way to the music, DVD and games markets achieved for their biggest releases. I immediately agreed that this was a good idea and that official 'Launch Dates' for the biggest titles would be supported by Waterstones – to the astonishment of those present, and to the annoyance of the likes of WH Smith who were now in a corner and had to reluctantly agree. This led to the most anticipated titles being launched with a bit more of a bang over the next few years, culminating in the midnight releases of the later Harry Potter titles which saw snakes of children queuing round the block of their local Waterstones, Borders and Ottaker's stores at midnight at the beginning of the official publication day.

This stance elevated me instantly into being seen as someone who was reasonable and prepared to consider and accept decisions that benefitted the whole trade ahead of my own company's particular interest. It earned me trust and respect from the outset and may have been a factor in me being elected as president of the Booksellers Association a few years later.

What the rest of the BA Council didn't realise was that I had noticed that WH Smith, who had a central warehouse and distribution centre in Swindon, were getting these books delivered to them well in advance of the advertised publication date and were turning them around rapidly to send them to their individual stores. By contrast, Waterstones had no such facility at the time and had all our books delivered by the publishers directly to each individual store. The lead time was later and, as a result, WH Smith consistently had the biggest new releases out on sale ahead of us. The new embargo date proposal slammed that door shut for the titles that mattered and had the bonus of being good for the trade and marketing new books. So, it wasn't entirely altruistic of me.

Avoiding the most obvious beartraps

The first few weeks in a new industry can be tricky, and there are a few hidden beartraps that need to be avoided.

The music industry is fairly fierce and quick to judge, and reputations can be built over many years and shattered pretty quickly. Comparing it to the publishing industry, when I was made Product Director of HMV, I would be faced with questions like, 'Who is the drummer on the third album by X?' If I didn't know the answer, I would be berated with remarks along the lines that I was not fit to be given the job with my crap music knowledge. In the same role for Waterstones, and new to the book world, I would be asked, 'Have you read X (book)?' and if my answer was no, the response would be, 'Oh, you should. I really think you'd enjoy it.'

Back to the music industry and an invitation to a record company dinner in the Oxo Tower restaurant where the entertainment included Lionel Richie playing the piano and singing to the room. Pretty cool. I was sat opposite Sharleen Spiteri and next to her was the new MD of Our Price, a competitor and important chain of record shops at the time. He had just joined from outside the music business and this was his first industry event. Sharleen asked him where he was from and he told her at length about his company, his background and himself. Eventually he asked her where she was from. 'Me? I'm from Texas,' she said, surprised he didn't recognise her as their lead singer. 'Gosh, you've come a long way,' said the Our Price MD, and his reputation was tarnished ever so slightly from that moment on.

Don't try and kid the specialists

Word gets round. The communities in your industry are smaller than you think and in publishing the author community, as you can imagine, is close-knit and far-reaching. There have been a few neophytes who have put their foot in it over the masculine virtues of George Eliot, but this tends not to be a cardinal sin. On being introduced to the wonderful author Sarah Waters at my first Waterstones conference, I asked her which store she worked in. Mortified.

On joining Waterstones, I discovered that our marketing director had been on a live panel with a best-selling crime author and the sometimes-feisty novelist had rather dismantled my colleague when she had tried to defend Waterstones from accusations of dumbing down and so forth. I was rather amazed to discover that, as a direct result, all the author's books had been de-ranged from Waterstones' stores, in a rather petty act of vengeance. I went to an industry awards dinner shortly after starting the job and spotted the author as the event was breaking up. I carted a bottle of wine over to their table, introduced myself, and suggested we have a drink together and find out what had been going on and what we needed to do to put it right. Cue explanations and apologies on both sides – including the author's admission that the effect of not having their books in Waterstones' stores was much more devastating than they had expected (clearly before Amazon had reached their current dominance). I took them through how our overall ranging strategy really wasn't dumbing down the stores – in fact, quite the reverse – and told them we would, of course, put their titles back into our stock. They acknowledged this and were relieved. It was such an easy thing to put right as I had had no personal responsibility for Waterstones up to that point or personal involvement in the author's accusations. Correcting the mishap was also firmly in the company's interests – not having this author's books in stock did not reflect well on us. The news of this rectification and the establishment of my reputation for not only being pragmatic and reasonable, but also prepared to sort out knots that had taken hold, went quickly around the agent and writer communities close to this particular author.

Trade associations and bodies

Trade associations are important but it's worth considering what they stand for and represent as well as how they operate. The official music charts have been around since the fifties with various methods of capturing sales data from a sample selection of record stores and extrapolating it to represent the whole market. It took over forty years, but in the nineties, the British Association of Record Dealers (BARD) formed a separate company to pool their data provision to the companies producing the official music charts and charged around a seven-figure sum for providing the data that enabled their existence. This was then carved up according to market share between the retailers. Realisation that they were the data provider for an asset being exploited by another party led to a great example of the benefit for all by collective action.

The BA Council were a long-established representative body for book retailers, but we had little or no connection with the Publishers Association trade council who were a similar body of publisher representatives. The CEOs of the two associations met but this was a little like the civil servants having the relationships while the politicians never had any formal route for dialogue. As a result, I suggested that we form a Publishers Association/Booksellers Association Liaison Group where the major players on each side of the industry could meet to identify and solve the bigger issues for the sector such as logistics, returns, marketing, etc. This was approved, we set it up, and I was elected as the inaugural co-chair with a publisher CEO as the other. This immediately gave me authority with my peers and access to all the CEOs of the major publishers and influential independents. I was Product Director of Waterstones at the time, not CEO or MD, but the perception across the publishers was different and I was the person to speak to.

Of course, you are acting in your own company's interests, but these often do align with the industry's welfare without necessarily damaging your commercial benefit. It may suit you to keep confidential areas which do give you an advantage over your competitors but there are others where the greater good for the industry overrides your own, often when this may be short-lived. Sustainability and the environment would be one, as the very essence of publishing is pulling down trees to provide paper to print books and ship them all over the world. Digital books, print on demand, distribution efficiencies and reducing the level of returns are all factors that are industry-wide initiatives that would be influential and beneficial. Ensuring the industry is more inclusive for authors, agents, publishers and booksellers is also a priority across race, class, ability and even regionality. This would widen the market considerably and deliver commercial benefits for book sales and also the resulting IP that may create content in other media.

Meeting others is always an opportunity – as Daniel Priestley says, 'You get what you pitch for, and you're always pitching.'[45] Everybody that you meet may be a future employer, employee, supplier, client, partner or advocate. They may not be able to help you but they may well know someone who can. Julia Leckey, former founder and CEO of brand consultancy Honest, is passionate about this:

> 'The number one thing is the power of your network. It fuels your business, your potential employees of the future, or if you need any expertise on NED or mentoring on any different facets. You are supposed to know everything about everything, but you don't, so having access to the right expertise is key. I met David Roche via my network when I reached

into it for advice. Wherever you are, know and understand who is around you – you are on stage and a life-changing opportunity could be found in a room of strangers any moment.'

Julia is clear that you can meet your next and best client at an awards ceremony or even when you are on holiday. It's you who the relationship is about and it's you who are the bridge to securing this potential new partnership. If you are a new CEO you need to be out and about, be friendly, energetic and enthusiastic and inspire others to take an interest. Building the relationship is the critical element rather than selling the pitch. Providing the relevant information and responding to queries with no agenda can be the best tactic if the relationship is built on solid ground and is unconditional. As Julia says:

'The test is, would they be interested enough in the conversation to stay for three drinks with you (coffee or G+T)? One means little, two shows an interest, but three demonstrates a commitment beyond the necessary – a wish to share their valuable time with you. Spending time with you adds value to others and their agenda.'

When I joined the publishing industry, my natural connections with the trade were through the BA Council and the publishers' sales teams. Having co-founded the PA/BA Liaison Group, I got a taste for extending my reach and knowledge into other branches of the sector such as academic publishing and literary agents, and generally at CEO level. Literary agents were a fun part of the industry and could be counted on for a good lunch and slightly indiscreet gossip. The old-fashioned word 'clubbable' could have been used for many of them. I enjoyed the company of several key agents and got to understand much more about the book trade from the point of view of the author and agent. This was slightly unusual for chain booksellers at that particular point in time but proved very useful further down the line.

Several years later, I was on the board at HarperCollins Publishers and was trying to drive 'special sales' through non-traditional channels. My team had some major successes, such as McDonalds buying vast quantities of Michael Morpurgo books to give away with sales of its Happy Meals. These initiatives saw low percentage margin but high volume and, therefore, sizeable amounts of cash being paid to, in effect, market our titles to a new audience. They in turn might become fans of the author and start buying the backlist. What's not to like? On one occasion, our very talented Special Sales Manager, Vikki Van Someren – who has gone on to significant success as co-founder/ co-CEO of The Bike Shed in London and Los Angeles – was mystified because she had set up an amazing deal, but the editor of the author who it was built on had said that their literary agent had turned it down. I knew the agent well from my lunches as a bookseller in years gone by and called her to explain how this really was a no-brainer that would benefit her author massively. Her reaction taught me loads. She had never received a call from the HarperCollins editor or been presented the opportunity. My call was the first she had heard about it and it sounded great! When I confronted the editor for turning down the opportunity and blaming the agent that she had never called, she burst out, 'It's my job to defend the author from these sorts of things that devalue their work!' It has often been an uphill struggle to drag the publishing industry into a wider and more mainstream audience.

Looking outside your industry for lateral learning

There is no reason why you should restrict your circle to those in your industry. The best thing about many business courses is the people you meet and contacts you make from other industries. We all face similar, if not the same, problems but don't necessarily tackle them the same way. Learning lessons from other sectors can be extremely enlightening and how others in lateral businesses go about solving similar problems can produce lightbulb moments.

I recently stood down as chair of BookBrunch, which is an online news service for the publishing industry. They are a small player relative to *The Bookseller* which is the long-standing and largest publishing trade magazine.

The Bookseller has the cash and resources to put on large conferences and awards dinners for hundreds of attendees to supplement their revenue from subscriptions. We had a handful of freelancers and needed to find additional revenue that did not require large amounts of resource or investment and also sat comfortably with, and would ideally enhance, our brand. We decided to launch a series of BookBrunch Breakfast Briefings that would be by invitation only and would aim at C-suite attendees from our best corporate subscription customers in the publishing industry. This would be a round table, intimate conversation with around twenty to twenty-five people under Chatham House rules.

I invited leading figures in industries that had some association with, or influence on, the invited audience and I found it remarkably easy to persuade speakers to attend gratis and give a talk and Q&A for an hour. Picking people who were writing a book or due to have one published made the job even easier. If they had recently resigned or just left their big role, they tended to be more indiscreet and more interesting. The list included Lord Tony Hall, Director General of the BBC; David Abraham, CEO of Channel 4; Kwame Kwei-Armah, Artistic Director at the Young Vic; Stephen Garrett, film producer and founder of Kudos; Chris Hirst, CEO of Havas; Kathryn Viner, Editor-in-Chief at *The Guardian*; and Baroness Martha Lane Fox. The events themselves were relatively easy to put on and attracted sponsors who were willing to not only pay to be associated, but also give over their board-room and provide a continental breakfast for those attending. The events themselves were well attended and enhanced our brand and reputation enormously and the list of previous speakers itself attracted new speakers that I contacted. Being in connection with such an illustrious list has done me no harm either.

Preparation for such events as a speaker is an interesting one. Asking politicians to speak for ten to fifteen minutes before a Q&A tends not to be a problem. Perhaps this is par for the course wherever they go, and they have people to prepare an appropriate patter for that particular audience. Offering an 'in conversation' option is often more popular, particularly if you are prepared to share the sort of initial questions so they won't be surprised. Supplementary questions are always fair game, and the aim of the game is not to trap them into a mistake, but to draw out some information or anecdote that is out of the ordinary.

There is an anecdote that I heard about Harold Macmillan, the UK Prime Minister from 1957–63, that, though possibly apocryphal, is food for thought. The story goes that he was giving a speech at a dinner and used some speech cards to ensure that he was prompted to include all the items that were relevant to that audience. The speech went well and received a good reception. When he exited the room, Macmillan left the speech cards on his seat and one of the audience members turned them over to take a look at his notes. To his astonishment, the cards were blank. Rather than look the polished speaker who required no notes, Macmillan opted to be seen as the speaker who had written the speech specifically for this event and this audience rather than delivering the same old speech that he parroted night after night to different groups.

The value (and sweetness) of formal recognition

Receiving recognition from the trade and your peers is always nice but, as with many awards, can be subjective and/or political. It's traditional to say that such awards mean nothing until you win one. I had a sweet and sour experience in the book trade when I was given the Personality of the Year, which was at that time the big one at the trade awards. Unfortunately, I was on gardening leave at the time, having had a slightly acrimonious exit from Waterstones when I handed in my notice to join rival Ottaker's as CEO. The terms of the gardening leave were strictly enforced and that included banning me from attending the lavish awards ceremony where I was to be presented the trophy. As I couldn't attend in person, I had to give a pre-recorded acceptance speech from my garden at home on video. A little sad, but it was a great feeling to win, especially as I had burned my bridges well and truly with HMV Group (Waterstones' owner) and they, in turn, had succeeded in outbidding the Ottaker's MBO and were set to be their new owners. I was on gardening leave with no job to go to.

The value of industry recognition showed its face, however. Borders book chain won an award on the same evening and their general manager at the time sent the glossy brochure featuring all the award winners to his boss in the US. As a direct result, I was brought to Borders' attention, contacted by them and started a dialogue which led to several meetings and the formal interviews at the Borders HQ in Michigan. On the day that my gardening leave expired, I was announced as the new CEO of Borders UK & Ireland. It is often said that the strict terms of gardening leave are nigh on impossible to enforce, and I gather that even the antagonistic faces at HMV Group gave a shrug of impressed surprise that I had resolved the tricky position that I had found myself in so favourably and in such quick time. I'm glad to also say that there have been a few great awards evenings that I have been able to attend and accept awards at since then, as well as a wonderful day at the University of Central Lancashire to accept an honorary degree for services to the UK book industry. It's both lovely to be recognised and good for your career prospects too.

Keynote takeaway

Being a key person of influence in the trade certainly has benefits, not only personally, but also for your company. It will attract the best people to your company and help retain those that are already there. It will encourage investment in what you are trying to do. And it will ideally improve the industry to be more efficient, sustainable and inclusive as a result.

ELEVEN

CEO Spotlight

*Navigating media relations with
grace, wit and PR wizardry*

'By making one of many slightly off-colour remarks
he is prone to relate at public functions, David
Roche managed to offend much of his audience...'
— *Private Eye*

This last section covers another important area –
the media. This may be either trade, regional,
national or international, but may be seen or heard
by people in your own company and your competitors, those who work with you who we have touched
on in the last few chapters, or the end consumers on
whom your business relies. Your relationship with
the media, and your skill in dealing with them, will
have an influence on how you and your company

are portrayed to all these important groups. Yes, it's important to walk the walk and provide the example to those who surround you, but the media provide the platform for recognition and allow you to do this on an altogether different scale.

The perils of getting it wrong

Though strictly speaking it was at an industry dinner, Gerald Ratner provided a perfect example of how an inside joke could be grabbed by the media with catastrophic consequences. He was CEO of his eponymous chain of jewellery stores and was giving a speech at the Institute of Directors in 1991. In his speech he described the jewellery sold in his stores as 'total crap' and described their earrings as 'cheaper than an M&S prawn sandwich, but probably won't last as long.' When this was reported in the media, the chain's sales collapsed, and Gerald Ratner had to resign as CEO. Further, the chain ended up being forced to rebrand itself as 'The Signet Group' to distance itself from the reputation from this one joke that it could not shake off. The public will put up with a lot of things but being called stupid, as Ratner inferred his customers were here, is one thing that they will not accept or forgive.[46]

No matter how behind closed doors speeches may appear to be or if Chatham House rules are supposedly

*Gerald Ratner thirty years on from the
press reaction to his speech*

in place, there's really no such thing as guaranteed confidentiality. In Ratner's case, he had made the same joke on prior industry occasions, but this time had a journalist from the *Daily Mirror* in the room, the UK was in recession and times were tough for the sort of punter who shopped at Ratners. This was a spicy story to report.

I learned a big lesson after presenting an award at a top industry charity do, the Nordoff Robbins Silver Clef lunch. This was an incredibly glitzy, annual affair with a very deserving cause that typically had an emotional speech given by the mother of one of the kids who was a beneficiary of the charity's work. This would pull the heartstrings of everyone there and was then followed by an auction which might have a guitar signed by a music legend which attracted stellar bidding along the lines of '£100,000 to you, Elton. Eric, do I hear £110,000?' It was always an extremely well-attended function, with more than a smattering of rock and pop royalty and the likes of Posh and Becks.

HMV used to sponsor the International Award and it was my job to get up and announce the winner and present the award. This had happened for several years and the modus operandi was I would research how many number one singles and albums the winners had achieved and give a short and rather bland speech and introduce them. In 2001 I attended my final Silver Clef lunch, as I had already announced that I was leaving HMV to move to Waterstones and this was probably my last music industry event. Frankly, I was in celebratory mood and a little worse for wear by the time the awards were being presented, and I had been doodling various letter combinations on the back of the awards programme. When the International Award was due, I did my standard intro format announcing the winner but ended, 'She's also a gay icon, but not because her name is an anagram of "You Like Minge"… Ladies and gentlemen, Kylie Minogue!' This, of course, went down like a lead balloon with a sizeable part of the audience, and I quite rightly received an almighty bollocking from the CEO of Kylie's record company, EMI, as getting the stars to give up their time to attend was difficult enough without insulting them when they did show up. I apologised in suitably grovelling fashion and Kylie was very magnanimous about it. I understand that the sponsors were restricted from giving speeches when they presented awards in the years following this. However, *Private Eye* picked up the story a while later and quoted this and another line I gave at an after-dinner speech at a trade dinner in Dublin as, '…one of many slightly off-colour remarks he is prone to relate at public functions'. Fair play, and I guess there are worst things to be known for, but it's a boorish stain and a note of caution. Know your audience before you go on and tailor what you say accordingly. Only say things that you would not mind being repeated in the media.

Being careful is one thing, but being overly dull is another. If you never say anything contentious or answer any questions, then the media will lose interest in you. You are not a Politician with a capital P (though, of course, you do need to be political).

The debate about a more charismatic CEO who has perhaps come from a marketing background versus the grey accountant CFO turned CEO is an old one. There is a level of balance between risk and reputation and I think it would not have taken much insight to guess that Gerald Ratner's speech carried a *code red* reputational risk to his company.

If it's fraught with danger and has potential down-sides, why give speeches or talk to the media at all? Because when done well, it can also do both you and your company the world of good. It can put you on the map and elevate your company's reputation as the leader in your market. Becoming a key person of influence in your industry is necessary to be considered for the top jobs going. Part of this is to become the go-to person for the media when they want a comment on industry related, big news stories. There are several things that you need to do to be considered for this:

- Always respond in a timely fashion – the media has traditionally worked under fairly strict diary imperatives owing to print deadlines and TV and radio slots and everyone loves a scoop.

- Always give quotes on the record and attributed to you – there may sometimes be some contention and not everyone may agree with you, but it's always more interesting and gains respect than a nameless quote.

- Answer the question – you may have distinct points that you wish to include in your response, but it's always better to answer the question before segueing into your agenda. Nobody likes the obvious avoidance that is so commonplace among politicians nowadays.

- Say something interesting! You are being asked as an expert, so stating what is obvious to every lay person who may be watching, listening to or reading hardly portrays you in a magic cloak of insight. Here is where some contention and risk may come in, but if you explain the reason for your opinion, people will take notice.

It's no surprise when watching talented debaters showing off their craft that the case can seem done and dusted after the first side has completed their case for or against the motion, only to reverse your decision once the second side has had their turn. Most media situations that you face as a CEO are likely to be more one-sided with you being given a free hand to state your case.

As with everything else, it's about relationships. There was a time when a reporter in the trade media wrote a slightly slanderous piece about a colleague's exit that relied on guessing what we thought of them and stating it was seen as good riddance internally. No effort had been made to verify this or get a quote and the journo's own prejudices were projected onto others as a result. I saw this as both lazy and unacceptable and complained to the editor. The complaint was not so much what was said, it was the way the reporter had gone about researching and verifying the real story rather than their assumed – and preferred – version of it.

Doing this from a position where we had a relationship of trust and relative openness rather than a defensive, flat-bat protectiveness added weight to the argument. I was mad keen at sport at school and played for every team I could; I understood that my consistent application allowed me to throw a sickie with no problem when the compulsory inter-house cross country run was due. There is an equal and opposite reaction to shouting, 'Wolf! Wolf!' I know others who have flown off the handle with the trade press on a regular basis and set them up on a war footing, stopping the corporate subscription based on a perceived slight. I never saw this approach work particularly well, and even if it's done in the name of hard-working staff whose efforts are not recognised, it shows a weakness to me rather than a strength.

Writing a book is another way to endorse your credentials as an expert in particular areas. And if you've reached this far, I'd like to believe you're coming around to my way of thinking! In authorship today there is a tendency to be more plain-spoken and straightforward than there used to be. The number of book titles with the word 'bullshit' in (number of asterisks used varies) is growing rapidly, always with the intention of deviating from the business bullshit bingo that corporate speak promotes and to tell it how it is. Search 'bullshit' on Amazon under 'books' and even just under 'business, finance and law' books if you don't believe me. Chris Hirst, CEO of Havas had enough success with his recent book, *No Bullsh*t Leadership: Why the world needs more everyday leaders and why that leader is you* to now be publishing a follow up called *No Bullsh*t Change: An 8 step guide for leaders.*[47] Lucy Kellaway, co-Founder of Now Teach, used to write a column in the *FT* for many years that poked fun and pricked the balloon that was management pomposity and jargon. In her book *Sense and Nonsense in the Office: No theories, no flow charts, no big words* she debunks the worst examples of business speak, and it is the business book for those of us who are not business book addicts.[48] It recognises the banality and boredom that can be associated with work and the fact that most people are just not very good managers or leaders.

Doing your homework and proper preparation

I was asked to speak at a conference on the theme of the Spoken Word at the Rose Theatre in Kingston upon Thames many years ago. I accepted, assuming that I just needed to mug up a bit on audiobooks, but that I knew the basic tenets and roughly what I would say. Luckily, I checked a week or so before the event to see who the other speakers were and the agenda. To my horror, the conference was on 'The Power of the Spoken Word' and my fellow speakers were actress Dame Janet Suzman on the power of the spoken word in the Arts, *Times* journalist and political speechwriter Philip Collins on the power of the spoken word in the Media, and an eminent Professor from Oxford University on the power of the spoken word in Education and Academia. I had been lined up and agreed to speak on the power of the spoken word in Business.

Aaaah. Ah.

I decided that attack would be the best form of defence, and that irony was a good sledgehammer to drive the message home. I did my entire delivery using a totally over the top PowerPoint presentation, embellished with the whizziest of transitions and animations, which demonstrated exactly how *not* to do it. It went down pretty well, and I felt I had dodged a bullet. The lesson was well learned: give enough time to really read and understand the brief, the audience and the other speakers.

Never be tempted to wing it with public speaking.

Know what you want to say and always rehearse it out loud to yourself (see the note earlier about rehearsing conference speeches with your senior leadership team, as appropriate). The hearing yourself and what you are planning on saying out loud is the must.

Of course, there are times when the media want to speak to you because they have something that you would prefer them not to have – news of poor results, a leak of intended strategy such as closing parts of your company, or perhaps even some scandal that threatens a reputational risk to the organisation. The temptation to go into denial or try and muffle the story or get angry and threatening can be strong but these are inevitably the wrong tactics. Most journalists are very used to handling this approach and, in fact, it's the equivalent of blood in the water for investigative sharks.

If it's true, then it needs to be faced and the best method may be to provide a fuller picture in order to enable the journalist to write a better story. This gives you the opportunity to provide context and a background that takes the sting or extremity out of the original story which may have been pieced together from scraps. Try and also pair the bad news with some good news which may originally seem unrelated but can be a balancing factor. You're shutting down a division because of economic factors affecting the whole market, but you are investing in a new facility in the North which will service a new and growing sector and provide employment. You can also qualify what can be used or not, but the knowledge they have may wash the rest of the story in a form of conditioner. Most large organisations will have some form of crisis communication plan but how you act and lead in this situation will be critical and hiding behind the comms expert who will be trying to flat-bat the media is not the best look. I've been called 'straight talking', 'frank', 'tougher than most' and even that I have 'a laugh like a pantomime baddie' and am 'certainly not a shy, sensitive flower.' I'd take that compared to being vanilla, non-committal and evasive.

Fake news?

Of course, social media is a slightly different kettle of fish. It's media, but it's more like a public conversation and very high-risk owing to its gladiatorial nature. Not just for businesses and their leaders, but for anyone. Jon Ronson's 2015 book *So You've Been Publicly Shamed* clearly takes the reader through how anyone can get on a plane as an unknown and get off a few hours later as the hated focus of an outraged mob.[49] A careless joke on social media can lead to complete vilification.

The last few years, particularly since the 2016 EU Referendum, have seen the binary nature of society come to the fore – people are clearly right or wrong and there's no in-between. Game shows and reality TV have democratised the decision-making – you, the public, gets to decide yes or no with a text and the 'X' will light up and the buzzer sound. It's the Emperor's thumb up or down to decide the gladiator's fate, but where we all get to be the emperor. It's not easy out there, only it's easier to be tough online, and in email, to an extent. I can't help feeling that people are nowhere near as brave or robust in real life. There's a short video doing the rounds on social media of two dogs barking fiercely and brandishing their teeth at each other, with just a glass door between them. With the door ajar, one of the dogs trots to the other side to a bowl of water sitting beside the second dog and takes a drink. It then returns back to the original side of the glass door and the ferocity between the two resumes.[50] That's social media for you. Or some of it.

Of course, we now have Artificial Intelligence (AI) to contend with too, and the world is wrestling to discover how to ride the upside while protecting us from the dangers. What is clear is that the capability for disinformation will rise excrementally – and that's not a typo. Every day is now April 1st.

Our gullibility needs to be on guard, at maximum alert. The 2024 US Presidential election will be the first where fake photos and facts will become a standard play in the process, and it may make the procedure during and following the 2020 election look as smooth as silk.

The other key recipients of the bad news that they will read about in the media are the relationships we have already reviewed earlier in this book. What will they feel when they read / see / hear it and what can be done to pre-empt that? This may well be different for affected employees compared to the board or investors / shareholders, who don't like surprises but may be relieved when the published story turns out to be better than expected (if they were pre-warned, perhaps with an even worse scenario).

It's worth remembering that providing interesting, unusual and newsworthy stories makes the job of the journalist easier. Providing press releases that reflect interesting trends or stats that can be extrapolated as stimulating and important shifts in the market can make your news far more thought-provoking than it might be in isolation. How you place this information is also a variable and the relationship you have with any individual journalist or media outlet can be considered when you believe an exclusive is worth more than maybe lesser coverage across a wider base. This may also build you brownie points with that journalist, which you may need to cash in at some point in the future.

Remember, you are the ambassador for your company but it's your reputation on the line as well. What is your go-to origin story that gives you the right to be where you are and to be passionate about what you do? Stick closely to that and the rest may just follow. It's relatively easy to get help that can be transformational and it escapes me why anyone with doubts in this area doesn't do so.

Keynote takeaway

'All the world's a stage' and the stages of your development are to get to be 'full of wise saws and modern instances' as soon as you can and with the benefit of experience and support.[51] Understanding the media, when and how to use it, why you wish to and what you hope to get out of it, and preparing properly for it, are all vital. If in doubt and with the opportunity, write it out and sleep on it. See if it makes sense in the morning. Actually, that excellent advice applies to most things.

Conclusion: From CEO Apprentice To Master

*Unleashing your lasting legacy
in the business world*

'I am not afraid of an army of lions led by a sheep;
I am afraid of an army of sheep led by a lion.'
—Alexander the Great

This book has been all about relationships and how they are key to achieving success, both for you and the company you work for. As can be seen with any team sport or activity, if everyone understands what they need to do, pulls together in the same direction, and tries their hardest for the good of the team, the likelihood that they will achieve great things improves dramatically compared with a few talented individuals doing good things in isolation. In fact, there can sometimes be high-achieving soloists who are toxic to the team and only care about hitting their personal goals. Common wisdom would suggest the good of the whole is more important and these people should be jettisoned – or perhaps found a role that suits this strength.

The role of the CEO has changed over the last ten years – there is even less time to think, less acceptance from customers for mistakes and wildfire reactions on social media to amplify any public-facing issues. What is consistent is the criticality and reality of dealing with other people and handling relationships. It also encourages reflection on your own thoughts and actions. There is no single or simple 'one size fits all' answer that can be applied in specific situations. All of us are different and may respond in a variety of ways. We may appear to react well or give that impression when, in fact, we are deeply upset. The art is to adapt and react to what is in front of you.

I apply both coaching and mentoring to first-time CEOs. As I mentioned earlier, I often find the critical breakthrough in problem solving for the client happens as a result of relating a story of something vaguely similar that happened to me along the way; it's quite typical to get to the end of a particular anecdote and find the client nodding away, having had a lightbulb moment. Not because what I did or didn't do in the story was the answer, but the parallel just jogged something in their awareness of their own situation which provided the insight that they needed. This sounds a little like luck, but it happens far too frequently to be just down to that. I hope that some of these experiences have the same effect on you when reading this book.

The combination of coaching and mentoring that I use is not necessarily favoured by coaches, and some mentors I know are excellent at what they do but they have no coaching training or experience. I realised that the combination of my professional coaching experience and qualifications, added to my twenty-eight years of board level experience, is a powerful combination. I can best explain the benefits of the combination like this. I have been lucky enough to have scuba-dived at many beautiful locations around the world, and a few years ago I enrolled in a freediving course to learn how to dive without an air tank. This was inspirational and worked as a result of a perfect blend of both coaching and mentoring. I wanted and needed to be told what to do by an expert, but I also needed to have my limiting beliefs removed in order to imagine – and truly believe – that I actually could do it. Within three hours I was holding my breath underwater for three-and-a-half minutes, and a day later I was freediving down to 20 metres. This result was, to me, staggering – even if it was, as I was told, typical for people who go through the same course. I have found first-hand that in business this powerful blend of coaching and mentoring can deliver staggering results too.

According to an article by Mike Ettore in *Forbes*, 'Research from the Corporate Executive Board (CEB) estimates that 50% to 70% of executives fail within eighteen months of taking on a role, regardless of whether they were an external hire or promoted from within.'[52] Hopefully this book will help those who read it to fall on the successful side of the line. Or at least that they seek out the vital support that an independent coach/mentor can provide. Being receptive to coaching tends to decline over time – we all know the sort of experienced CEO who is averse to feedback, whether that is advice or criticism of the most constructive type. They have to make a conscious decision to keep sharp and gain new skills by inviting counsel.

One must-read text for all new first-time CEOs and the best short read that I've seen that helps on the subject is the 'Letter to a newly appointed CEO' by Ian Davis in the McKinsey Report in June 2010.[53] It gives ten pieces of advice following an imaginary discussion over dinner on ways to try and ensure successful leadership transition. I recommend reading this above any of the multitude of business books on the subject.

Having said that, here are my own ten actions to try and give yourself better odds of success and which address the key areas that result in failure. These are the ones to remember if you forget everything else:

1. **Get a professional, independent coach/mentor.**
   This is probably the most important guarantor of success, as it will help with managing your own doubts about yourself and providing you with

trusted support that will alleviate the new lone-liness associated with the top position. It's for high achievers and should be compulsory for all first-time CEOs.

2. **Learn to understand yourself and what drives you.** You are the one constant in all your relation-ships and you need to be aware and in control of the elements that you know you handle well and the ones you need to work on.

3. **Set up an induction process that includes soft skill problem reviews, as well as meeting people.** Ask the chair and board to tell you where their concerns lie, as getting a new CEO can be seen as the catalyst for the change that they want, but it helps to let you know what these include.

4. **Don't be afraid to seek further training.** This should be for both yourself, your senior leader-ship team and identified high-fliers who will be the leaders of tomorrow – it helps to be trained in leadership rather than learning on the job or from untrained bosses you may have had in the past.

5. **Get out and talk to people at all levels and understand and own the culture.** From the board to the receptionist, and from your EA to the fur-thest outpost you operate in, everyone will have an opinion and something to contribute and you will be surprised how quickly these coalesce into a pattern. The history and traditions will be an important factor in how you implement change.

6. **Ensure you have a relationship of equals and trust with your chair and board.** This is a critical one to establish from the beginning. They hired you as the best person that they have selected for the job and to improve the company's performance both now and for the future. That means they need to work as closely as they can with you to help you deliver this success rather than sit with report cards assessing, marking and being critical of your performance. Calling out any such behaviour early on is much more likely to establish the desired pattern going forward.

7. **Ensure you have a positive, effective and diverse senior leadership team.** Hire the best people possible – better than you if you can, and not in your own likeness. Knowing your weaknesses (and strengths) will help here. Cultural fit is important, but so is diversity, and it's your job to knit together the cohesive and high-performing team that you wish them to become.

8. **Define, communicate, inspire and live a culture of ownership and risk-taking innovation.** Everyone needs to understand the overall direction the company is going in and where you want them to get to. Clarity around values is critical, as is the use of the word 'why' at many stages. How you communicate and enthuse the company is supported by how you act and how risk-taking and failure is handled, as well as success. Be an empathetic, modern leader, not a bully.

9. **Concentrate on the big picture, resource your teams to deliver and measure progress.** You are no longer a functional head and you can't do your senior leadership team's jobs for them. You can manage them to success and plan how the pieces fit together, but you need to lead the vision, the process and the company so that the machine runs as well as possible.

10. **Manage the change.** Change is the new normal and is coming at us faster than ever before, so needs to be embraced. A change in outcomes needs to start with a change in beliefs, so understand where you are now and what you need to do on a daily basis to deliver small-step, incremental improvement in the right direction rather than massive 'all or nothing' projects.

There is one further tip that doesn't make this list, but is worth having up your sleeve. Julia Leckey offers great advice on many leadership areas, but the most practical of all may be that, 'If people don't value you or your talent on any level, don't hang on in there, gather up all your magic and experience and move on as quickly as possible. If you can't make a difference and you're not enjoying it, then quickly move on.' Johnny Fewings, serial media CEO, told me that it is critical to be aware of whether you are *genuinely* accepting of a particular change and what is going on, or are you happier with avoidance. There is no halfway house.

What happens if you achieve great success – how do you best cope with it and what sort of legacy would you like to leave behind?

We can't all be the big, household names at the top of the *Sunday Times* Rich List, but we can be good enough to inspire others and make things better. The widely travelled and respected correspondent John Simpson tweeted recently that:

> 'Out of the 200 or so world leaders I've met over fifty years, I've only really liked and admired three for their human qualities, even though many of the others have been admirable as politicians: Nelson Mandela, Vaclav Havel and Volodymyr Zelensky.'[54]

The odds of leaders having admirable human qualities would seem slim, but things have changed over half a century. Aiming to be a better boss than the ones that you have had is probably a reasonable place to start, followed by leaving the company in a better state than when you inherited it. Setting up those who work for you to have successful careers and fulfilling their careers has to be the other.

Having a work/life balance is more critical for some than others, and many entrepreneurs would say that there is an unavoidable, all-encompassing period where work dominates your life almost to the exclusion of everything else. The founder of Microsoft,

Bill Gates, once said, 'I never took a day off in my twenties. Not one.'[55] On the other hand, I've worked with and for others who have an extraordinary ability to shut down outside the office, though their radar remains on at all times and scans for contacts, information, ideas and opportunities that may be relevant and come to their attention during the off time.

Finally, get enjoyment from paying it forward. Today's middle manager and CEO are tomorrow's CEO and chair. As we get to the pinnacle of our career, and certainly as it slides past, helping others be the best they can becomes one of the most enjoyable things you can achieve. If you are looking for a legacy to leave behind you, then living, breathing examples of success are a pretty good one. Being a non-exec director and a coach/mentor requires many similar skills, and I trained as an exec coach initially to hone those skills that would make me a better chair. Having decades of experience around a board table is also invaluable to others who are starting out, and having experienced failure as well as success is of immense value – as long as you recognise the reasons and lessons learned.

Being a key part of a successful business that can change the lives of your consumers, customers, staff and families for the better can be a fabulously fulfilling experience, as well as a highly stressful one. Remember that it's not all on your shoulders to deliver everything, but also about helping others to give of their best.

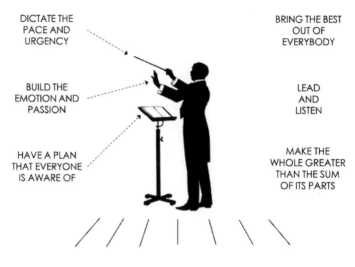

DICTATE THE
PACE AND
URGENCY

BRING THE BEST
OUT OF
EVERYBODY

BUILD THE
EMOTION AND
PASSION

LEAD
AND
LISTEN

HAVE A PLAN
THAT EVERYONE
IS AWARE OF

MAKE THE
WHOLE GREATER
THAN THE SUM
OF ITS PARTS

How to perform as a CEO

The orchestra conductor is the only one of the ensemble who doesn't deliver a note of what the audience experiences. How wonderful it is to lead everyone around you to a magnificent, collective performance with these three tools that you control: inspiration, empathy and sensitivity.

So, pick up your baton… Tap, tap, tap. And go…

Notes

1 GM Matthews, 'Imposter phenomenon: Attributions for success and failure', paper presented to the American Psychological Association, Toronto, 1984

2 R Charan, 'Ending the CEO succession crisis', *Harvard Business Review* (February 2005), https://hbr.org/2005/02/ending-the-ceo-succession-crisis

3 P Sellers, *Being There* (Lorimar, 1979)

4 BBC News, 'Guy Goma: "Greatest" case of mistaken identity on live TV ever?', BBC News (10 May 2016), https://youtube.com/watch?v=e6Y2uQn_wvc&t=36s

5 R Balla, 'Man mistaken for IT expert during live interview says he will sue BBC over lack of royalties', Sky News (28 August 2023), https://news.sky.com/story/man-mistaken-for-it-expert-during-live-interview-says-he-will-sue-bbc-over-lack-of-royalties-12949458

6 DL Maddocks et al, 'The assessment of orientation following concussion in athletes', *Clinical Journal of Sport Medicine*, 5/1 (1995), 32–35, https://pubmed.ncbi.nlm.nih.gov/7614078

7 R Mavity, *The Rule Breaker's Book of Business: Win at work by doing things differently* (Piatkus, 2013)

8   J Armstrong (creator), *Succession*, TV series (HBO, 2018–2023), www.hbo.com/succession

9   N Gaiman, 'The Neil story (with additional footnote)', *Neil Gaiman Journal* (17 May 2017), https://journal.neilgaiman.com/2017/05/the-neil-story-with-additional-footnote.html

10 C Da Silva, 'Michelle Obama tells a secret: "I have been at every powerful table you can think of... They are not that smart"', *Newsweek* (4 December 2018), www.newsweek.com/michelle-obama-tells-secret-i-have-been-every-powerful-table-you-can-think-1242695

11 Tina, 'Impostor syndrome: 3 surprising benefits of it' (Mentessa, 2022), www.mentessa.com/posts/3-surprising-benefits-of-impostor-syndrome

12 OnePoll research on behalf of NerdWallet, conducted between 24 November 2022 and 30 November 2022: C Campbell, 'Over three quarters of UK business leaders have experienced impostor syndrome', *NerdWallet* (13 December 2022), https://nerdwallet.com/uk/business/imposter-syndrome

13 BBC News, 'Who is Liz Truss? Political journey of UK's shortest-serving prime minister', *BBC News* (20 October 2022), https://bbc.co.uk/news/uk-politics-63331087

14 J Kruger and D Dunning, 'Unskilled and unaware of it: How difficulties in recognizing one's own incompetence lead to inflated self-assessments', *Journal of Personality and Social Psychology*, 77/6 (1999), 1121–1134, https://doi.org/10.1037/0022-3514.77.6.1121

15 K Kay and C Shipman, *The Confidence Code: The science and art of self-assurance – what women should know* (HarperBusiness, 2014)

16 V Young, *The Secret Thoughts of Successful Women: Why capable people suffer from the impostor syndrome and how to thrive in spite of it* (Crown Publishing Group, 2011)

17 E Partaker, 'How to cure imposter syndrome', LinkedIn post (January 2023), https://linkedin.com/posts/eric-partaker-5560b92_how-to-cure-imposter-syndrome-activity-7023589211920318464-xhHK/?originalSubdomain=re

18 M Cousens, 'Gareth Cheeseman self-motivation speech' (24 February 2017), https://youtube.com/watch?v=uXi-nWuzAG4

19 W Leatham, 'Harry Enfield – you didn't wanna (picnic)' (17 July 2017), https://youtube.com/watch?v=eH56UOjDQ4A&t=32s

20 CA Hildebrand et al, 'Predicting CEO success: When potential outperforms experience' (SpencerStuart, 2020), https://spencerstuart.com/research-and-insight/predicting-ceo-success-when-potential-outperforms-experience

21 M Djikic et al, 'Opening the closed mind: The effect of exposure to literature on the need for closure', *Creativity Research Journal*, 25/2 (2013), 149–154, www.tandfonline.com/doi/abs/10.1080/10400419.2013.783735

22 E Catton, *Birnam Wood* (Granta Books, 2023)

23 K Power, 'Birnam Wood by Eleanor Catton review – hippies v billionaires', *The Guardian* (3 March 2023), www.theguardian.com/books/2023/mar/03/birnam-wood-by-eleanor-catton-review-hippies-v-billionaires

24 Center for Presidential Transition, *The 2020-21 Presidential Transition: Lessons learned and recommendations* (Center for Presidential Transition, January 2022), https://presidentialtransition.org/publications/2020-21-lessons-learned

25 quoteresearch, 'Everybody has plans until they get hit for the first time', *Quote Investigator* (25 August 2021), https://quoteinvestigator.com/2021/08/25/plans-hit

26 The Myers-Briggs Company, 'The Myers-Briggs Type Indicator® (MBTI®) assessment' (The Myers-Briggs Company, no date), https://eu.themyersbriggs.com/en/tools/MBTI?gclid=Cj0KCQjwl8anBhCFARIsAKbbpyQSlNoYMLD1WUeCII-QNf-vyDPYQS2ty1guJ2LQxzYPMLHh4hdGLjMaAtSkEALw_wcB

27 R Williams, 'Why CEOs fail, and what to do about it', *Financial Post* (21 July 2010), https://financialpost.com/executive/careers/why-ceos-fail-and-what-to-do-about-it

28 P Maddox, 'Time after time. Why new CEOs fail so often' (Just Open Leaders, 2021), https://justopenleaders.com/time-after-time-why-new-ceos-fail

29 For a diagram depicting the process, see D Roche, 'The CEO Winner's Circle process' (Grey Area Coaching, 2023), https://greyareacoaching.co.uk/wp-content/uploads/2023/03/PRODUCT-ON-A-PAGE-POA.png

30 J Jubelirer, '"Everyone needs a coach" Bill Gates and Eric Schmidt' (November 2013), https://youtube.com/watch?v=XLF90uwII1k

31 TJ Saporito, *Inside CEO Succession: The essential guide to leadership transition* (Jossey-Bass, 2012)

32   TJ Saporito, *Inside CEO Succession: The essential guide to leadership transition* (Jossey-Bass, 2012)

33   S Sandberg, *Lean In for Graduates* (Knopf, 2014)

34   S Bayley and R Mavity, *Life's a Pitch: How to sell yourself and your brilliant ideas* (Bantam Press, 2007)

35   Admin, 'Quality quote by Henry Ford – American businessman' (Streamline, no date), https://streamline.business/quality-quote-by-henry-ford-american-businessman

36   J Galvin, '4 ways to build a stronger culture in a tight labor market' (Vistage, 2019), https://vistage.com/research-center/business-leadership/organizational-culture-values/20190925-culture-is-important-how-to-make-yours-stronger

37   Generally attributed to Peter Drucker: MC Learning, 'Culture eats strategy for breakfast' (MC Learning, no date), https://managementcentre.co.uk/management-consultancy/culture-eats-strategy-for-breakfast

38   A Rhoden-Paul et al, 'I've been forced out over Partygate report, says Boris Johnson', *BBC News* (10 June 2023), www.bbc.co.uk/news/uk-politics-65863267

39   R Branson (@richardbranson) 'There's no magic formula…', tweet (23 April 2015), https://twitter.com/richardbranson/status/591218817675702274?lang=en-GB

40   Deloitte, *2023 Global Chief Procurement Officer (CPO) Survey* (Deloitte, 2023), www2.deloitte.com/content/dam/Deloitte/us/Documents/consulting/us-2023-global-chief-procurement-officer-survey.pdf

41   SM Wagner, 'Supplier development and the relationship life-cycle', *International Journal of Production Economics* 129 (2011), 277–283, https://doi.org/10.1016/j.ijpe.2010.10.020

42   A Smith, 'It's official: News Corp. to split into 2 companies', *CNN Money* (28 June 2012), https://money.cnn.com/2012/06/28/news/companies/news-corp-split/index.htm

43   T Arango, 'How the AOL-Time Warner merger went so wrong', *New York Times* (10 January 2010), https://nytimes.com/2010/01/11/business/media/11merger.html

44   M Randolph, *That Will Never Work: The Birth of Netflix by the first CEO and co-founder Marc Randolph* (Endeavour Publishing, 2019)

45 Daniel Priestley (@DanielPriestley), 'You get what you pitch for…', tweet (4 April 2018), https://twitter.com/danielpriestley/status/981412237117132801

46 G Hiscott, '"Mr Crap" Gerald Ratner battles back after losing everything to be millionaire', *The Mirror* (2 April 2021), https://mirror.co.uk/news/uk-news/mr-crap-gerald-ratner-battles-23843472

47 C Hirst, *No Bullsh*t Leadership: Why the world needs more everyday leaders and why that leader is you* (Profile Books, May 2019); C Hirst, *No Bullsh*t Change: An 8 step guide for leaders* (Profile, June 2023)

48 L Kellaway, *Sense and Nonsense in the Office: No theories, no flow charts, no big words* (Financial Times Management, 2000)

49 J Ronson, *So You've Been Publicly Shamed* (Picador, 2015)

50 r/AnimalsBeingDerps, 'Internet Fight', Reddit post (2022), www.reddit.com/r/AnimalsBeingDerps/comments/10328a2/internet_fight

51 W Shakespeare, *As You Like It* (c. 1599)

52 M Ettore, 'Why most new executives fail – and four things companies can do about it', *Forbes* (2020), https://forbes.com/sites/forbescoachescouncil/2020/03/13/why-most-new-executives-fail-and-four-things-companies-can-do-about-it

53 I Davis, 'Letter to a newly appointed CEO', *McKinsey Quarterly* (1 June 2010), https://mckinsey.com/featured-insights/leadership/letter-to-a-newly-appointed-ceo

54 J Simpson (@JohnSimpsonNews) 'Sadly, out of the 200 or so…', tweet (12 July 2023), https://twitter.com/JohnSimpsonNews/status/1679053783282728960

55 R Dancsi, 'I never took a day off in my twenties', *Psychology Today* (8 October 2021), https://psychologytoday.com/gb/blog/dear-life-please-improve/202110/i-never-took-day-in-my-twenties

Acknowledgements

There are so many people to thank over the years for giving me the chances, knowledge and support in my career. I learned from everyone I worked with to a degree and, in some cases, also learned how I did not want to work. Interestingly, many of the examples of how not to do it came from people who had amazing strengths in other ways – I guess very few, if any, are the complete package. Thanks to you all for putting up with me.

For support with this book, a big thanks to early readers, contributors and providers of anecdotes. Particular thanks to Martyn Gibbs for writing the foreword and to the following contributors: Dan Oakey, David Kohn, Sherrie Asgari, Glen Ward, John Seager, Jake Pugh, Salma Ibrahim, Eugene Buckley, Leticia Rita,

Roger Mavity, Stephen Bayley, Stephen Carter, Alice Edgcumbe-Rendle, Julia Leckey, Tuula Ingman, My Ly, Jon Glen, Kerr MacRae, Johnny Fewings, Richard Charkin, Susie Nicklin, Arnivan Sen, David Rothwell, and Marlene Hauser. Not all made the final book, but all helped shape the final result.

Special thanks to Danny Butcher for allowing the use of his excellent illustration that kicks off Chapter One.

At my publisher, Rethink Press, thanks to Lucy McCarraher, Joe Gregory, Anke Ueberberg, Kathleen Steeden and Lisa Cooper for their diligent, professional and invaluable support and help in arriving at the final version of the book. It was a painless and enjoyable process with a lot of sage advice!

For my coaching and mentoring expedition, thanks to Trudi Ryan, Sue Kennedy, everyone at The Coaching Academy, Adrienne Kaemmerlen, Daniel Priestley and all at Dent KPI for help and encouragement along this career path.

And finally, thanks to my wife Johanna for encouraging me to pivot into coaching and mentoring alongside my work on boards. I originally investigated this path to make me a better non-exec and chair, but I have grown to be rather awed by its magical power and effect, and love working with enthusiastic clients and seeing them soar. Everyone should experience the immediate and pragmatic benefit that a coach and mentor's positive support provides!

The Author

 David Roche is a professional coach and mentor at Grey Area Coaching, and works with first-time CEOs across many sectors. He studied psychology at Durham University and has a professional qualification in hypnotherapy.

David is Chair of London Book Fair and the writing agency New Writing North. He also works as a consultant with startups entering the book industry and lectures at NFTS. His first book, *Just Where You Left It,* was published by Unbound in 2017.

David was previously CEO of Borders & BOOKS etc, Product Director of both Waterstones and HMV, and Group Sales and Marketing Director of HarperCollins Publishing. He was also President of the Booksellers Association and a trustee of BookTrust. David has received several industry awards and in 2017 was awarded an Honorary Fellowship from the University of Central Lancashire for services to the UK book trade.

🌐 www.greyareacoaching.co.uk

🔗 www.linkedin.com/in/davidroche